Together Is Better

Teacher's Resource Module

Lynn Bryan
Charolette Player

CONSULTANTS

Ron Benson

Susan Elliott

Diane Lomond

Ken MacInnis

Kim Newlove

Liz Stenson

GENERAL EDITOR

Kathleen Doyle

Prentice Hall Ginn Canada
Scarborough, Ontario

Canadian Cataloguing in Publication Data

Bryan, Lynn, 1942-
Together is better. Teacher's resource module

(Collections 5)
ISBN Nos.
0-13-099885-0   Atlantic Edition
0-13-099886-9   Ontario Edition
0-13-099887-7   Western Edition

1. English language – Study and teaching (Elementary).
2. Language arts (Elementary). I. Player, Charolette. II. Title. III.
Series: Collections (Scarborough, Ont.).

PE1121.T63 1997 Suppl.   428.6   C96-932578-9

Prentice-Hall, Inc., Upper Saddle River, New Jersey
Prentice-Hall International, Inc., London
Prentice-Hall of Australia, Pty., Sydney
Prentice-Hall of India Pvt., Ltd., New Delhi
Prentice-Hall of Japan, Inc., Tokyo
Prentice-Hall of Southeast Asia (PTE) Ltd., Singapore
Editora Prentice-Hall do Brasil Ltda., Rio de Janeiro
Prentice-Hall Hispanoamericana, S.A., Mexico

ISBN Nos.
0-13-099885-0   Atlantic Edition
0-13-099886-9   Ontario Edition
0-13-099887-7   Western Edition

Publisher: Kathleen Doyle
Managing Editor: Carol Stokes
Content Editor: Janis Barr
Copy/Production Editor: Norma Kennedy/Debbie Davies
Production Co-ordinator: Stephanie Cox
Permissions: Angelika Baur
Design: Word & Image Design Studio Inc.
Illustrations: BLMs 7,8,21: Vesna Krstanovich

Printed and bound in Canada by Best Book Manufacturers
1 2 3 4 5 6 BBM 2002 2001 2000 99 98

CREDITS

BLM 12: "The Sneeze" by Sheree Fitch and "Anxious" by Miriam
Waddington. Appeared in *Til All The Stars Have Fallen,* copyright
©1989. Kids Can Press, Toronto.
BLM 13: "Hot Wheels and Hoops" © Marsha Scribner, freelance
writer for the Wainwright Star Chronicle/ May '94. Reprinted with
permission.
BLM 16: "The Pitcher's Arsenal" reprinted with permission – The
Toronto Star Syndicate. Copyright: Knight Ridder Newspapers.
Covers pp. 1, 4, 105, 106, 107, 112, 115:
The Hundred Penny Box published by Puffin Books; illustrated by Leo
and Diane Dillon. *Baseball, Snakes, and Summer Squash* published by
Wordsong (Boyds Mills Press); drawings by Paul Birling. *A Bad Case
of Robots* published by Puffin Books; illustrated by Peter Utton.
How Come the Best Clues Are Always in the Garbage? published by
Kids Can Press; cover illustration by Pat Cupples.

Sources for resources on page 5

Links to Media
- Canadian Learning Co., 95 Vansittart Ave., Woodstock, ON; N4S
  6E3; 519-537-2360; 1-800-267-2977
- International Tele-Film Enterprises, 301-5090 Explorer Dr.,
  Mississauga, ON; L4W 4T9; 905-629-3133; 1-800-561-4300
- Magic Lantern Communications, 775 Pacific Road, Unit 38;
  Oakville, ON; L6L 6M4; 905-827-1155; 1-800-263-1717
- National Film Board. Atlantic Canada: 1-800-561-7104; Quebec:
  1-800-363-0328; Ontario: 1-800-267-7710; Western and
  Northern Canada: 1-800-661-9867
- New Vision. 1132 Hamilton St., Ste. 100; Vancouver, BC V6B 2S2
  604-689-9549; Fax: 604-683-9369.

Links to the Information Highway
- The CD-ROM Shop, 204 Ontario Street, Toronto, ON., M5A 2V5;
  1-800-999-9756; 416-368-5000; Fax: 416-366-9008
  Distribute: *The Amazing Writing Machine; The Canadian
  Encyclopedia Plus; Dogs; Earth's Natural Resources*
- Core Curriculum Technologies/Software Plus, #1-12760 Bathgate
  Way, Richmond, BC, V6V 1Z4; 1-800-663-7731; Fax: 604-273-6534
  Distribute: *The Print Shop Deluxe; Encarta; The Canadian
  Encyclopedia Plus; Imagination Express: Oceans*
- Educational Resources, 38 Scott St. West, St. Catharines, ON,
  L2R 1C9; Canada: 1-800-565-5198; Ontario: 905-988-3577;
  Fax: 1-800-311-4600
  Distribute: *Creative Writer; The Amazing Writing Machine; Print Shop
  Deluxe; Earth's Natural Resources; Encarta; The Canadian
  Encyclopedia Plus; Imagination Express: Oceans*
- Educator's Choice Software Company, 29 Meadowview Drive,
  Bedford, NS, B4A 2C3; 902-452-6313; Fax: 902-832-0167
  Distribute: *Encarta; The Print Shop Deluxe* (Will take orders for
  any title.)
- Microsoft Canada, 320 Matheson Blvd. West, Mississauga, ON;
  1-800-933-4750
  Distribute: *Creative Writer 2; Dogs; Encarta*

ACKNOWLEDGEMENTS

Prentice Hall Ginn Canada wishes to express its sincere appreciation to the following Canadian educators for contributing their time
and expertise during the development of this teacher's resource
module.

Kathryn D'Angelo, Vice-Principal, Tomsett Elementary School,
Richmond, BC

Lori Rog, Language Arts Consultant, Regina Public Schools,
Regina, SK

Sandra Sutton, Teacher, St. Richard School, Mississauga, ON

Links to the Information Highway, page 5:
Debbie Miller, Teacher, École Van Walleghem School, Winnipeg, MB

Prentice Hall Ginn Canada would also like to express its
appreciation to the staff and students of Warden Avenue Public
School, Scarborough, Ontario, for their assistance with this
publication.

Contents

About the Unit

The selections and learning opportunities in this thematic unit focus on family relationships and working and playing with others.

UNIT FOCUS

This unit will help students develop concepts pertaining to
- **special moments and memories** within the context of special relationships with family, extended family, and friends.
- **team work** as experienced through group activities, sports, and games, with an emphasis on co-operation, team spirit, and relationships.
- **causes that count**, with a look at the concern of young people for our environment.

Throughout the unit, students will have many opportunities to
- make connections between the relationships and special activities presented in the literature in *Together Is Better* and those they experience with their own friends and families.

- use language for many purposes, most notably to
  - recount and narrate experiences.
  - reveal something about themselves.
  - persuade/convince others of a point of view.
  - gather and organize information.
  - question, reflect, and assess.
  - imitate/draw upon ideas, patterns, and presentational forms found in literature.
  - use conventions of spelling, capitalization, punctuation, and language usage.

LANGUAGE ARTS LEARNING EXPECTATIONS

As students participate in the learning experiences in the *Together Is Better* unit, they will meet expectations pertaining to the following:

Reading

Students will
- read a variety of fiction and non-fiction materials for different purposes—short stories, articles, poems, readers' theatre scripts, songs, picture books.
- explain their interpretation of a written work, supporting it with evidence from the work and from their own knowledge and experience.
- make judgements and draw conclusions about the content in written materials, using evidence from the materials.
- read independently, selecting appropriate reading strategies.

Writing

Students will
- communicate ideas and information for a variety of purposes and to specific audiences—journals, persuasive and informational letters, poems and songs, instructions, articles, definitions.
- use writing for various purposes and in a range of contexts to reflect on their thoughts, feelings, and imaginings.
- produce pieces of writing using a variety of forms.
- use correctly the conventions—spelling, grammar, punctuation.

Oral Communication

Students will
- express and respond to ideas and opinions concisely, clearly, and appropriately.
- ask and answer questions on a variety of topics to acquire and clarify information.
- contribute and work constructively in groups.
- use tone of voice, gestures, and other non-verbal cues to help clarify meaning when describing events, telling stories, reading aloud, making presentations, stating opinions, etc.

Visual Communication

Students will
- create a variety of media works—maps, timelines, cross-section diagrams, paintings.
- analyze media works—paintings, illustrations, maps, timelines.
- read independently, selecting appropriate reading strategies.

(See *Appendix 1* for specific indicators of each expectation.)

UNIT RESOURCES

Student Books

ANTHOLOGY

The *Together Is Better* **anthology** contains a range of fiction and non-fiction selections of both published and student writing. It is intended for instructional use in a whole class or group teaching/learning context.

GENRE BOOKS AND NOVELS

There are two **genre books** and two **novels** to provide sustained reading of longer prose pieces. They can be used in small group literature circles for book and novel study.

GENRE BOOKS

• *The Hundred Penny Box,* by Sharon Bell Mathis. This touching book-length story tells of a young boy's love for his great-great aunt. Michael's hundred-year-old aunt has a box of pennies, one for each of her birthdays, and a favorite pastime for Michael is listening to his aunt tell the story behind each penny.

• *Baseball, Snakes, and Summer Squash,* by Donald Graves. In this collection of free verse poems, Donald Graves provides a look at his experiences as a young boy at home and in school, most of them about his life after his family moved out to the country from their city apartment.

NOVELS

• *A Bad Case of Robots,* by Kenneth Oppel. This is a humorous story about a trio who get involved with a sensational machine—a robot that seems to know everything until things start to go wrong.

• *How Come the Best Clues Are Always in the Garbage?,* by Linda Bailey. In this mystery novel, eleven-year-old Stevie Diamond sets out to catch the thief who stole money donated to an environmental group. Stevie has many exciting and humorous adventures as she follows up on clues.

Strategies for using the genre books and novels can be found on pages 105–118 of this guide and in the book *Teaching with Novels, Books, and Poetry.*

Teacher Materials

The **Teacher's Resource Module** for *Together Is Better* presents teaching and assessment activities for each of the selections in the student book.

The **blackline masters** intended for use with this unit are included at the back of the Teacher's Resource Module. The blackline masters include masters that are additional activities and home link masters.

Learning Strategy Cards introduced in this unit are

1. Keeping a Personal Dictionary
2. Reading Words in Context
3. Learning to Spell Words
4. Getting and Keeping Track of Writing Ideas
5. Types of Questions
6. Personal Narrative
7. Diamante Poems
8. Two-Part Choral Reading
9. Making an Outline
10. Posters
11. Readers' Theatre
12. Persuasive Letter
13. Handwriting

These cards are available within the **COLLECTIONS 5 Teacher's Resources** as a pack of 62 cards. Templates for some cards are available on disk (compatible with Mac and IBM).

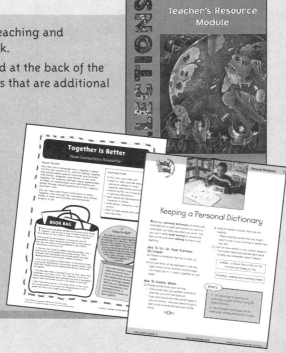

Read-Aloud Books

Choose a book to read aloud throughout this unit.
- Carrier, Roch. *The Basketball Player*. Tundra, 1996. 24 pp.
- George, Jean. *Who Really Killed Cock Robin? An Ecological Mystery*. New York: Dutton, 1971. 149 pp.
- Gilbreath, Frank B. and Ernestine Gilbreath Carey. *Cheaper by the Dozen*. New York: Bantam, 1975. 180 pp.
- Johnston, Julie. *Hero of Lesser Causes*. Toronto: Lester, 1992. 178 pp.
- Mathias, Beverley. *The Spell Singer and Other Stories*. London: Puffin, 1991. 152 pp.

Personal Reading

With help from the school librarian and the students, assemble a classroom library of books pertaining to relationships for students to browse through and choose for personal reading. The following books are suggested:
- Gaetz, Dayle Campbell. *A Sea Lion Called Salena*. Vancouver: Pacific Educational Press, 1994. 128 pp. Novel. Cdn. Average reading level.
- Hoffman, Mary. *Grace & Family*. London: Frances Lincoln Limited, 1995. Unpaginated. Picture book. Average reading level.
- Humber, William. *The Kids' Soccer Book*. Toronto: Somerville House, 1994. 64 pp. Non-fiction. Cdn. Average to challenging reading level.
- Korman, Gordon. *The Chicken Doesn't Skate*. Scholastic Canada, 1996, 192 pp. Novel. Cdn. Average reading level.
- McFarlane, Brian. *Hockey for Kids*. Toronto: Kids Can Press, 1994. 64 pp. Non-fiction. Cdn. Challenging reading level.
- Mathis, Sharon Bell. *Red Dog, Blue Fly: Football Poems*. New York: Viking, 1991. Unpaginated. Picture poetry book. Average reading level.
- Sadiq, Nazneen. *Camels Can Make You Homesick*. Toronto: Lorimer, 1985. 89 pp. Short stories. Cdn. Average reading level.
- Walter, Mildred Pitts. *Mariah Loves Rock*. New York: Bradbury Press, 1988. 117 pp. Novel. Easy to average reading level.
- Waterton, Betty. *Quincy Rumpel and the All-Day Breakfast*. Vancouver: Groundwood, 1996. 118 pp. Novel. Cdn. Easy to average reading level.
- Yee, Paul. *Teach Me to Fly, Skyfighter*. Toronto: Lorimer, 1983. 133 pp. Short stories. Cdn. Average reading level.

Links to Media

These videos relate to topics within the unit.
- *Best Friends*. Canadian Learning Co. 1987. 29 min.
- *Come Sit By Me*. Magic Lantern. 1992. 7 min.
- *The Marzipan Pig*. International Tele-Film. 25 min.
- *Paper Camera*. International Tele-Film. 1992. 25 min.
- *The Sweater (Le Chandail)*. NFB. 1980. 11 min.
- *The Wednesday Surprise*. Magic Lantern. 1992. 14 min.
- *Where Do I Fit In?* New Vision. 1991. 16 min.

Links to the Information Highway

Software such as that listed below can be used to extend learning on the topic or on selected learning outcomes of the unit.
- *The Amazing Writing Machine* from Broderbund: Template program; students can write/illustrate stories, keep journals, create essays/ reports, develop a database of penpals/key pals, and learn about four poetic forms. *Mac/Win 3.1 disk; Mac/Win CD-ROM*
- *Creative Writer 2* from Microsoft: A program of writing and drawing tools. Easy access to the Internet. *Win 3.1/Win 95 CD-ROM*
- *Dogs* from Microsoft: Information on 250 different breeds of dogs from around the world. *Win 3.1/Win 95 CD-ROM*
- *Earth's Natural Resources CD* by Clearvue: What government, industry, and communities can do to keep the environment clean. Plants and animals presented as natural resources along with the importance they play in a balanced ecosystem. *Mac/Win CD-ROM*
- *Encarta '97* from Microsoft: Multimedia encyclopedia integrated with user's word processor allows text, images, and sound to be incorporated in documents. *Win/Mac CD-ROM*
- *Imagination Express Series/Destination: Ocean CD* from Edmark. Ocean habitats, the roles of oceans in ecosystems and human impact on oceans. *Mac/Win CD-ROM*
- *The Print Shop Deluxe* from Broderbund: Three hundred graphics and thirty fonts for banners, newsletters, greeting cards, posters. *Mac/Win 3.5 disk*
- *The 1997 Canadian Encyclopedia Plus* from McClelland & Stewart: A current Canadian reference with illustrations, Quicktime movies, animation, sound clips, and maps. *Mac/Win 3.1 CD-ROM*

Note: Sources for these videos and software products are listed with the credits on page (ii).

Topic Focus	TOGETHER IS BETTER Anthology ⬥ = Canadian ⌒ = available on audio (student writing is indented)	Genre	Reading Level Range 3 4 5 6	COLLECTIONS 5 Genre Book Links
SPECIAL MOMENTS AND MEMORIES	⌒ ⬥ A Morning to Polish and Keep	picture story book	▪ at 5, • at 5	*Baseball, Snakes, and Summer Squash* by Donald Graves
	That Was Summer	poem		3 4 5 6 — • ▪ at 5
	⬥ Moments and Memories	anecdotes	• at 4, ▪ at 4–5	
	⬥ How I Got My Dogsled	picture story book	• at 4, ▪ at 4–5	
	⬥ Don't Just Sit There, Get a Hobby	short story	• at 4, ▪ at 5	
	⬥ Family Reunion	memoir		
	⬥ Whipping Cream	anecdotes		
	⬥ Camp-Out Disaster	poem		
PERSON TO PERSON	⌒ Shelter Folks	picture book story	• at 4, ▪ at 5	*The Hundred Penny Box* by Sharon Bell Mathis
	Offerings	poems		3 4 5 6 — • at 4, ▪ at 4–5
	⬥ Helping Hands	article	• at 4, ▪ at 5	
	⌒ ⬥ Working Out Problems	poem		
	⌒ ⬥ Dear Mrs. Hicks	letter		
	⌒ ⬥ Talk with Me	poem		
WORKING TOGETHER AS A TEAM	⬥ Hot Wheels!	article	▪ at 5, • at 6	
	⌒ ⬥ The Hockey Song	song		
	The Big Game	readers' theatre	• at 4, ▪ at 5	
	⬥ Team Sprit	acrostic poem		
	⬥ Hockey	poem		
	⬥ Teamwork	essay		
	⬥ My Baseball Game	personal narrative		
	⬥ Good Try	story		
WORKING FOR A CAUSE	⌒ The Last Dragon	picture book story	▪ at 5, • at 6	
	⬥ Last Chance for Cherry Tree Creek	short story	▪ at 5, • at 6	
	⌒ ⬥ Worldly Wise	poems		
	⬥ Our Environment	commentary		
	⬥ Pollution	poem		
	⬥ Animals	opinion		

Criteria for Reading Level Range

Key: The Reading Level Range is the independent level. The solid boxes indicate the overall readability. The dot indicates the range.

Factors that we considered:
- *concept load*: number and nature of new concepts, amount of exemplification, contextual support
- *language considerations*: vocabulary, sentence patterns, and complexity
- *writing style and tone*: familiar or unfamiliar, informal or formal
- *genre type and structure*: familiarity, predictability, and repetitiveness of the elements of the story or writing form
- *selection length*
- *classroom reality*: selections represent a range of abilities in a Grade 5 classroom

Factors that you may also consider:
- *familiarity*: each student's background knowledge and familiarity with the topic
- *student interest*: each student's degree of interest in and motivation for the topic and/or content of the selection
- *reading stage/level of the student*: whether he/she can read it independently,

COLLECTIONS 5 Novel Links	Other COLLECTIONS 5 Anthology Links	Other PRENTICE HALL GINN Links
	In Flanders Fields: The Story of the Poem by John McCrae (Unit 2) *book excerpt* The Great Blue Heron Diary (Unit 3) *diary* Heroine of Lunenberg (Unit 5) *true story* An Interview with Bing-Go the Clown (Unit 4) *interview* The Lotus Seed (Unit 5) *picture book story* Orangedale Whistle (Unit 5) *song lyrics*	Brian's Brilliant Career (L10) The Bush Telegraph (SUN11) Favorite Books (SS) Feelings (SUN10) The Golden Crane (SS) Marathon Runner (SS) Kerry's Keys (SUN10)
A Bad Case of Robots by Kenneth Oppel 3 4 5 6	An Interview with Bing-Go the Clown (Unit 4) *interview* Mirette on the High Wire (Unit 4) *picture book story* Sing to the Stars (Unit 4) *picture book story* Heroine of Lunenburg (Unit 5) *true story*	Barney (L9) The Golden Crane (SS) Hats Off! (SUN9) Kimo's Big Secret (SUN7) The Mystery of Fathers (SS) Ryan's Dog Ringo (L10)
	Ride the Shuttle! (Unit 3) *article* Behind the Scenes (Unit 4) *article* The Sacred Harvest (Unit 5) *article* Silver Threads (Unit 5) *picture book story*	Favourite Games Around the World (SUN10) Goalie (SUN10) The Hackers Club (S5) Morgan's Brainstorm (SS) Movie Magic (SUN10) The Mysterious Dr. Chen (SUN11)
How Come the Best Clues Are Always in the Garbage? by Linda Bailey 3 4 5 6	A Family for Minerva (Unit 3) *true story* A Children's Chorus (Unit 5) *declarations*	Operation Noble Creek (SS) Many Happy Returns: a Review of Recycling (L10) Earth in Danger (L10) Kay McKeever and the Owls (S5) Tears Are Not Enough (S5) A Wetland Home (SUN10)

Keys:

The COLLECTIONS 5 units referred to in the second last column are as follows:
Unit 2: *Tales—Clever, Foolish, and Brave*
Unit 3: *Weather, Wings, and Kite Strings*
Unit 4: *On with the Show!*
Unit 5: *Exploring Heritage*

Letter codes in the last column indicate the following Prentice Hall Ginn publications:
S5 = *Journeys: Springboards 5*
SS = *Journeys: Sail the Sky*
L9 = *Literacy 2000: Stage 9*
L10 = *Literacy 2000: Stage 10*
SUN7 = *Sunshine Books: Level 7*
SUN8 = *Sunshine Books: Level 8*
SUN9 = *Sunshine Books: Level 9*
SUN10 = *Sunshine Books: Level 10*
SUN11 = *Sunshine Books: Level 11*

with teacher guidance, with peer support, or in a listen-and-read approach only
- *reading strategy used*: the reading strategies suggested in the *Teacher's Resource Module* are intended to allow most Grade 5 students to enjoy and understand the selections
- *language level of the student*: whether or not the student's birth language is English

The following activities can be initiated over two or three days to
• launch student interest in the unit.
• provide a common base for class, group, or individual learning experiences.
• engage the students in sustained learning throughout the unit.
• establish a procedure for spelling workshops.

Read aloud a book

Choose one or more of the books on page 5 to read aloud to the class throughout the unit of study.

Set up a unit bulletin board

An ongoing bulletin board display could feature photographs of the students, examples of student writing, and other pieces of work students create throughout the unit. The unit title "Together Is Better" can be an overall heading for the bulletin board, with more specific headings being made from time to time for particular groupings of work displayed. Specific suggestions for student work displays are provided in the teaching plans for the selections.

Consider having a small group of students be facilitators for creating the display. This group would be responsible for such things as gathering their peers' work, arranging the pieces on the bulletin board in an organized and connected way, creating headings, and changing the display at an appropriate time.

Establish a writing area

Create an environment that supports process writing. Explain to the students that they can go to this area to write about topics they are interested in, to discuss their writing with you or one another, to consult reference sources, to find various writing materials, and to store their writing portfolios.

Involve the students in preparing the writing area by suggesting that they begin an author/illustrator chart and display. They can record the names of authors and illustrators encountered in this unit, list other books they have written/illustrated, and note any tips provided in the profiles after the selections. Students can also include ideas, tips, and models from the student writing pages.

Students can continue to add to their chart as they encounter new authors and their ideas in other units or as they develop their own ideas.

Use computers

Using available equipment and space, set up a computer learning centre. Allow students to choose from a variety of activities appropriate to their abilities and needs. Using the computer, students can write and illustrate personal stories and memories, journals, mini-books, fold-out books, personal dictionaries, or spelling lists. Some can be put on display and others taken home to be shared with family and relatives. Books they write can be loaned to the school library or another classroom. Included in the computer centre can be a variety of software related to the theme. Look for this symbol throughout the unit to find links to computers, other electronic media, and technical writing.

To reinforce learning between the home and the school,

- use the *Home Connections Newsletter*, Blackline Masters 1-2. Send these pages home at appropriate times during the unit.
- encourage students to bring resources from home, such as books, magazines, video cassettes, and computer games that pertain to relationships between family and friends. They can share these with classmates or include them in the classroom library.
- invite students to share with their families, caregivers, and friends favorite stories or poems they have read or written throughout the unit.
- look for the home link symbol  throughout the unit.

Plan for spelling workshops

Spelling strategies and activities are provided in eight selected teaching plans in the *Together Is Better* unit. In this unit and in subsequent units of *COLLECTIONS*, the focus is to integrate spelling with reading and writing.

Teachers can

- choose a few **high utility words** to focus on each week, perhaps in collaboration with the students. Refer to high utility lists compiled by people such as Ves Thomas, Mary Tarasoff, Rebecca Sitton, and Edward Fry.
- have students select some **personal words** they would like to learn to spell. They can draw these words from various subject areas, difficult words encountered in personal writing, words related to the theme, or other words that interest them. *Keeping a Personal Dictionary*, Learning Strategy Card 1, can be used to help students choose and keep a record of their words.

- use or adapt the **unit spelling words** compiled from prose selections. These words highlight particular patterns, structures, and strategies, and include early level and challenge lists. (See *Appendix 3*, page 154, for an overview of unit spelling words.)
- use the spelling **blackline masters** provided with the selections to produce word cards for sorting and study. (See *Language Workshop—Spelling*, page 16 of this guide.)

For each group of spelling words, there are specific activities in the *Language Workshop— Spelling* section of the teaching plan for the selection.

A Morning to Polish and Keep

In this picture book story by Julie Lawson, a family shares a special day together, filled with memories to keep.

Anthology, pages 4-9 **Blackline Masters 3 and 22**
Learning Strategy Cards 2 and 3

Learning Choices

LINK TO EXPERIENCE

Tell About a Special Time

Brainstorm Fishing Words

READ AND RESPOND TO TEXT

READING FOCUS

- read a variety of fiction and non-fiction materials for different purposes
- STRATEGY: **read and paraphrase**

Assessment

REVISIT THE TEXT

mini LESSONS

READING
Read Words in Context
- use their knowledge of elements of grammar and oral and written language structures to understand what they read

WRITING
Language Workshop — Style
- select and use words to create specific effects
Language Workshop — Spelling
- compound words; ow and _le patterns

Assessment

VISUAL COMMUNICATION
Share Memories
- create a variety of media works

Assessment

LINK TO CURRICULUM

LANGUAGE ARTS
Publish a Classroom Book

Play a Word Game

SCIENCE/THE ARTS
Create a Display or Mural

SCIENCE
Diagram the Life Cycle of a Salmon

Key Learning Expectations

Students will
- read a variety of fiction and non-fiction materials for different purposes (**Reading Focus, p. 11**)
- use their knowledge of elements of grammar and oral and written language structures to understand what they read (**Reading Mini Lesson, p. 12**)
- select and use words to create specific effects (**Writing Mini Lesson, p. 13**)
- create a variety of media works (**Visual Communication Mini Lesson, p. 14**)

LINK TO EXPERIENCE

Tell About a Special Time

Discuss with the students how we enjoy remembering special times we have shared with others, such as weddings, birthdays, vacations, family outings, and so on. Ask them to recall a special time with their family or friends and describe a memento of the experience that helps them remember it. They might suggest photographs, videos, postcards, T-shirts, seashells, and store-bought souvenirs.

Have the students join with a partner to share a story of a special time and tell about any keepsakes they have from the experience.

Brainstorm Fishing Words

Ask students to brainstorm words or phrases that could be associated with a fishing experience. List their responses and then categorize them in a web on chart paper.

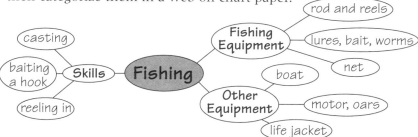

Tell the students that they will be reading about a family on a fishing trip and to jot any words or phrases they find in the story to add to the web after the reading.

READ AND RESPOND TO TEXT

Reading Focus

Using a **read and paraphrase** strategy, pairs of students can read the story together or listen to the *COLLECTIONS 5* audio version. They can take turns reading or listening to parts of the selection, pausing at specified points to retell what happened in the section they just read, supplying as many details of the plot as possible.

The organizer shown suggests possible pause points in the story and hints that students might use to guide their retellings. You may wish to write it on the board or an overhead transparency.

Pause Point	Retelling Hints
page 5: "They'll come as soon as your mind is on something else," I said.	- a starlit sky - into the boat - Island of Second Chances - check the tackle box
page 6: It was gone, just like that—hook, line, and sinker. And my salmon with it.	- sunrise comes - Amy catches a fish - Michael shouts - Amy loses fish and rod
page 8: We were having fresh salmon for supper.	- watching the whales - Michael hooks fish - Amy gives encouragement - Michael catches more than fish
page 9: It's a bit hazy around the edges, but when I give it a polish it comes out bright and clear and shining.	- Amy finds something special to keep - Amy remembers the day

Get Ready to Read

Put the title of the selection on the board and ask students to speculate on how someone might be able to polish and keep a morning.

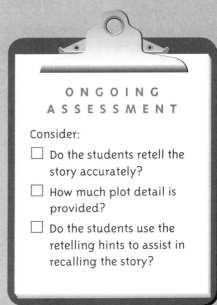

ONGOING ASSESSMENT

Consider:

☐ Do the students retell the story accurately?

☐ How much plot detail is provided?

☐ Do the students use the retelling hints to assist in recalling the story?

Reader Response

Students could
- hold a conversation about the story, discussing questions such as:
  - **How did Amy feel after she lost her fish and rod?**
  - **Did she hold a grudge against her brother? How do you know?**
  - **How did the family feel toward each other? What did they do that showed how they felt?**
  - **Why do you think this day was so special for Amy?**
- design questions to ask their classmates about their most unusual or favorite outing with family or friends.
- write in their journals about a personal experience this story reminds them of.
- add fishing words and phrases to the web.
- talk to a family member about a favorite fishing trip or other special memory and draw a picture about it.

Reading

Read Words in Context

Learning Strategy Card 2

To help students acquire strategies for figuring out unknown words, you can
• use Learning Strategy Card 2.
• work through examples from the selection.

Have the students look through the selection to choose three words whose meanings they are unsure of. List these words on the board. Choose one of the words to illustrate how clues to the meaning of a word can be found in the sentence in which the word appears and in sentences preceding and following it. For example, for the word "teeming," read the paragraph on page 5 and point out the context clues that will help predict its meaning:

"...we were the only living things on the water. But beneath...
...Salmon were making...
...Spiny-finned rockfish darted...
...Moon jellyfish floated..."

Ask students to predict the meaning of "teeming," and have a volunteer confirm their prediction in a dictionary.

Individually or in pairs, students can choose three words from the list and use context clues from the selection to predict their meanings. Suggest that they check their predictions in a dictionary.

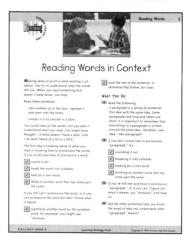

Students could refer to Learning Strategy Card 2 for review and further practice.

> It is important for readers to look at information before, near, and beyond the word to help them understand its meaning.

Writing

Language Workshop — Style

Blackline Master 3

Write the following cloze sentences from the story on the board and ask the students to suggest verbs for the blanks.

> At the edge of the marsh, we _____ along the beach, over pebbles, barnacles, and broken shells.
>
> Dad started the engine. It _____ and _____, then eased into a smooth running hum.
>
> Dad guided the boat carefully round the point, and then we _____ into the Strait.

Record their suggestions for each blank; for example,

> ...we   skipped   along the beach...
>   walked
>   ran
>   tip-toed

Discuss how each verb conveys a different image to the reader and why it is important to writers to choose precise verbs to describe action when they are writing.

Then compare the students' suggestions with the author's choice and talk about which verb they prefer and why.

The students could:
– jot verbs they like from the story in their journals.
– revisit a piece of writing and substitute more precise verbs.
– complete Blackline Master 3, *Action Verbs*.

 Assessment   See **Assess Learning**, page 15.

For **Language Workshop — Spelling**, see page 16.

Action Verbs

Replace the underlined verbs in these sentences with stronger verbs that convey a clear image for the reader.

John <u>said</u>, "Help me , I'm scared."

_____

Sally <u>cried</u> when the nurse gave her the needle.

_____

With the wind <u>blowing</u> and the rain <u>falling</u>, the family <u>went</u> for shelter to escape the violent storm.

_____

Write three sentences of your own in which strong and precise verbs are used.

_____

_____

_____

Now examine a piece of your writing and replace weak verbs with strong verbs. Share your edited changes with a partner.

Blackline Master 3

Visual Communication

Share Memories

Invite students to bring to school a memento of a past experience that is special to them. For those children who do not have a memento, have them draw a picture of something that reminds them of a past event they like to remember.

Invite each student to list information about the memento and the experience on a card. (The information can be written in point form.) Ask the students to tell the important facts of the experience and why the memento is important.

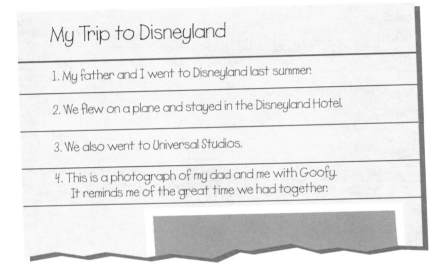

My Trip to Disneyland

1. My father and I went to Disneyland last summer.

2. We flew on a plane and stayed in the Disneyland Hotel.

3. We also went to Universal Studios.

4. This is a photograph of my dad and me with Goofy. It reminds me of the great time we had together.

Have students set up a display of their mementos/drawings and their cards. As they visit the display, encourage them to ask questions of each other to elaborate on their experience.

LINK TO CURRICULUM

Language Arts

Publish a Classroom Book

Students could write a memoir of a first experience, recalling that, in this story, the author experienced a number of firsts. Or they could write about a special experience with their own family or friends, perhaps building on the stories they have already shared in class.

Some students might like to use word processing programs to write and illustrate their stories. (See pages 5 and (ii) for more information.) The completed stories could be bound into a classroom book.

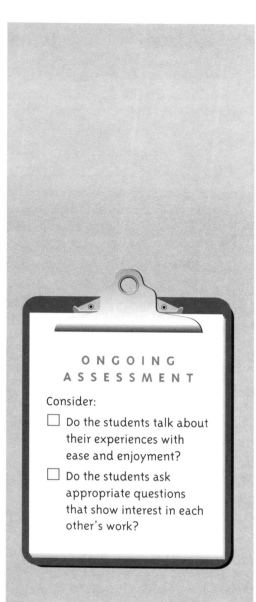

ONGOING ASSESSMENT

Consider:

☐ Do the students talk about their experiences with ease and enjoyment?

☐ Do the students ask appropriate questions that show interest in each other's work?

Play a Word Game

Groups of three or four students could create cards for a game of "Definitions," using words from the story. Have each group choose ten words, write each word on a card, and write a definition for each word on another card. Each group can play the game with their cards and then switch with other groups to play more games.

Science/The Arts

Create a Display or Mural

Recall with the students the sea creatures mentioned in the selection — barnacles, salmon, spiny-finned rockfish, moon jellyfish, and killer whales. Discuss where they think the story takes place.

Students could research these and other creatures that would share the same waters to find five interesting facts about each. Encourage students to access information through resources such as CD-ROMs and the Internet (by entering the keyword "sea creatures" in the search engine). (See pages 5 and (ii) for more information.)

The students could post their facts along with a drawing or picture of each creature.

Or, the students might like to take what they learn about the creatures and the ocean they live in and create a mural of life beneath the sea.

Science

Diagram the Life Cycle of a Salmon

Pairs of students could choose a kind of salmon and research its life cycle. Suggest that they share the results of their research in an illustrated diagram. Encourage the pairs to choose both Pacific and Atlantic salmon so they can compare the life cycles of these two groups of fish.

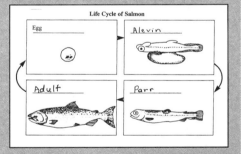

Life Cycle of Salmon

Egg   Alevin

Adult   Parr

A s s e s s   L e a r n i n g

Assessment

Writing (see p.13)

Use Blackline Master 3, *Action Verbs*, as a **work sample** to assess each student's ability to use strong verbs in their sentences to create a more precise image for the reader. Note whether they are able to use precise action verbs:

- at a practical level [1 - 4]
- at an application level:
  – in student written sentences [5 - 7]
  – to edit a piece of personal writing [8]

Rules for the Game of Definitions

1. Place all cards face down and mix them up.
2. Player 1 turns over two cards. If the player matches a word with its definition, the player keeps the card and plays again.
3. If there is no match, the player replaces the cards face down, and the second player takes a turn.
4. The game is over when all cards are picked up.
5. The player with the most cards wins.

Blackline Master 22

Explore and Discover

Use Blackline Master 22 to make overhead transparency cards and to reproduce copies for students to use.

Review the words by composing oral sentences using words students are unsure of. Suggest that they first group the words according to meaning, then into categories of their own choice.

Invite students to **share** their groupings using the overhead transparency cards. **Discuss** the common features and spelling patterns in the words, focusing on the "ow" and "__le" patterns and on compound words. Have the students suggest other words with the same patterns, or look through their own

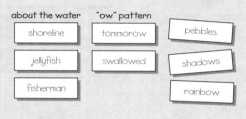

writing or books they are reading to find other examples. They can begin an ongoing wall **chart** to list words with selected spelling patterns.

Invite students to identify parts of words that might cause difficulties, and as a group, think of ways to remember the correct spelling.

Pretest

Administer the word list as a pretest, perhaps using the spelling buddy approach. Dictate the words, each time saying the word, using it in a sentence related to "A Morning to Polish and Keep," and then repeating the word.

Collaboratively correct the words. Show each word, asking students to put a dot under the letters they have spelled correctly and to underline the places where they had errors. Students can list the words they need to study.

Students who have few or no errors could
• study Theme/Challenge Words from the story.
• locate and practise challenging words from their own writing.
• play or create word games.
• act as spelling resource leaders for other students.

Students experiencing difficulty could
• be given fewer or less difficult words.
• study the Early Words and other pattern words related to them.

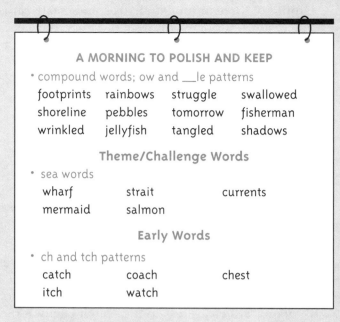

A MORNING TO POLISH AND KEEP

• compound words; ow and __le patterns

footprints	rainbows	struggle	swallowed
shoreline	pebbles	tomorrow	fisherman
wrinkled	jellyfish	tangled	shadows

Theme/Challenge Words

• sea words

wharf	strait	currents
mermaid	salmon	

Early Words

• ch and tch patterns

catch	coach	chest
itch	watch	

Study and Practise

Students could
• use Learning Strategy Card 3 to study words identified after the pretest.
• arrange their word cards from easiest to most difficult. For each of the five most difficult words, they first highlight the tricky part on the card and try to picture that part in their minds. They then close their eyes and spell the word aloud to a partner as they write it on their desk with their finger.
• work with a partner to build word crosses. The pair writes one of their list words in the middle of a sheet of paper. They then take turns adding words to it, either horizontally or vertically.

Post Test

Administer the post test. For those students who have an altered list, give the test at another time. Record the number of words each student spelled correctly and note the improvement since the pretest. Identify the types of errors the students made and use these as a guide for reteaching and study.

Spelling Buddies
Pair students of like abilities and have them be responsible for dictating words for both tests to each other. Spelling buddies can help one another in checking the pretest, and in their study and practise.

That Was Summer

This poem, by Marci Ridlon, is an invitation to remember some summertime experiences by recalling sensory images that are associated with the season.

Anthology, pages 10-11
Learning Strategy Card 4

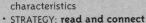
Learning Choices

LINK TO EXPERIENCE

Describe and Recall Smells

Graph Favorite Summer Activities

READ AND RESPOND TO TEXT

READING FOCUS
Assessment
• identify various forms of writing and describe their characteristics
• STRATEGY: **read and connect**

REVISIT THE TEXT

mini LESSONS

READING
Web Sensory Images
• read a variety of fiction and non-fiction materials for different purposes

WRITING
Use Questions to Develop a Writing Topic
Assessment
• produce pieces of writing using a variety of forms

VISUAL COMMUNICATION
Design a Collage
• create a variety of media works

LINK TO CURRICULUM

LANGUAGE ARTS
Create a Season Poetry Book

Create a Guessing Game

SCIENCE
Research Seasonal Changes

SOCIAL STUDIES/SCIENCE
Compare Seasons

Key Learning Expectations

Students will:
• identify various forms of writing and describe their characteristics **(Reading Focus, p. 18)**
• read a variety of fiction and non-fiction materials for different purposes **(Reading Mini Lesson, p. 19)**
• produce pieces of writing using a variety of forms **(Writing Mini Lesson, p. 20)**
• create a variety of media works **(Visual Communication Mini Lesson, p. 21)**

LINK TO EXPERIENCE

Describe and Recall Smells

Arrange students in groups and provide each group with three or four things to smell—a bar of soap, popped popcorn, cinnamon sticks, container of vinegar, sheet of fabric softener. Ask each group to smell the items and jot down words that describe each thing and anything else that comes to mind from the smells.

In a large group, have students share their words and ideas. Focus the discussion by asking:
• Are smells easy to describe? What words do we use?
• What is another way we use to describe smells? (comparison: It smells like...)

Ask students to talk about any personal experiences that have associations with distinct smells, such as roast turkey, chlorine, wet wool, cut grass, popcorn, spices, …

Graph Favorite Summer Activities

Have students brainstorm a list of activities they enjoy doing over the summer months and jot their ideas on the board. Their list may include such activities as swimming, bike riding, playing in the woods, building a fort, fishing, playing at the park, and so on.

Ask each student to choose a favorite activity from the list and tally their responses. Then work together to make a bar graph to show the top ten summer activities of the class. Have the students ask four or five questions that the completed graph answers.

Get Ready to Read

To establish a purpose for reading this poem independently, ask students what they think might be included in a poem entitled "That Was Summer." Have them read to check their predictions.

ONGOING ASSESSMENT

Consider:

☐ Do the students use the four-fold organizer effectively?

☐ Are the students able to synthesize information from the poem?

Reading Focus

Using the **read and connect** strategy, have the students read the poem independently. After each stanza, ask them to jot what they noticed about the pattern and the structure of that particular stanza. After they have finished, encourage them to read the poem again and jot any patterns they might have missed the first time. The following questions may help in guiding their observations:

• How did the stanza begin? How did it end?
• Did the author repeat words or sentences?
• Are there similarities among patterns used in all the stanzas?

The students could use a four-fold organizer to record their thoughts for each stanza.

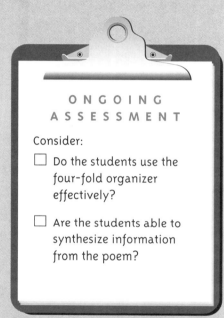

1. – begins with a question
   – uses word "remember"
   – asks two more questions
   – ends with "that was summer"

2. – begins with word "remember"
   – asks two questions
   – ends with "that was summer"

3. – begins the same as verse 2
   – asks two questions
   – ends with "that was summer"

4. – different beginning:
   "If you try very hard"
   – asks two questions
   – ends with "that was summer"

Reader Response

Students could
• talk with some classmates about whether they liked the poem and why.
• jot in their journals any personal memories that the poem reminded them of.
• with a partner, share the information they gathered and recorded in their four-fold organizer.

REVISIT THE TEXT

Reading

Web Sensory Images

A related homework project is to talk about, write about, and illustrate a favorite time of year. See *Home Connections Newsletter,* Blackline Master 2.

Have students revisit the poem to recall the smells of summer the author talks about. Use these to begin a web of sensory images of summer on the board or chart paper. Talk about how reading these words evokes strong images in our minds so that we are nearly able to smell what the author is describing. Ask students to brainstorm other specific images of summer that come from our other senses and add these to the web.

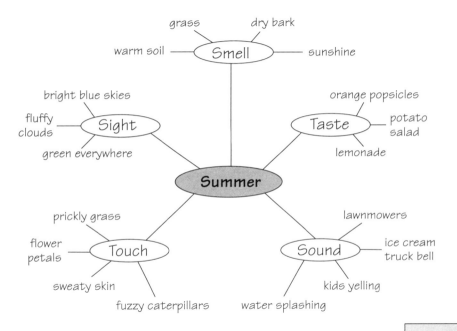

Students could then work in pairs to make their own webs of sensory images. They could choose summer or another season. Suggest that they look through books or magazines for pictures that will help them evoke images of their season. When they feel ready, ask them to write about the season using images from their web. They could write

• a stanza following a pattern from the poem, using any sense as the focus.

• a poem about a season using any form or pattern they wish.

• a description of a wonderful seasonal experience or day they had.

Remember the time
when you went for a swim in the lake
and there was no wind
and not a sound could be heard
and you just floated in the water
then after you moved you caused ripples
in the water?
Remember the smell of the green water
clean, clean, and cold?
That was summer.

Kala

Use Questions to Develop a Writing Topic

Learning Strategy Card 4

Recall with the students what a personal journal is and what it can be used for. Together, brainstorm a list of procedures and criteria for journal writing and post it in your classroom.

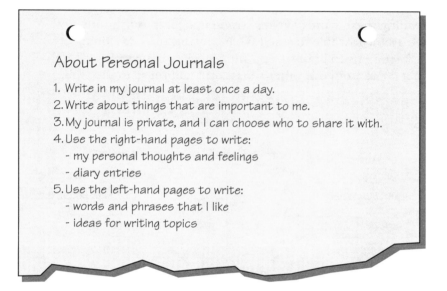

About Personal Journals

1. Write in my journal at least once a day.
2. Write about things that are important to me.
3. My journal is private, and I can choose who to share it with.
4. Use the right-hand pages to write:
   - my personal thoughts and feelings
   - diary entries
5. Use the left-hand pages to write:
   - words and phrases that I like
   - ideas for writing topics

 Some students may be interested in keeping a personal journal on the computer, using a journal template offered by programs such as *The Amazing Writing Machine*. (See pages 5 and (ii) for more information.)

To help the students develop ways of generating writing topics, use · Learning Strategy Card 4. You may choose to have some students try the suggested activities before asking each student to list several personal memories in their journal that they might like to write about; for example, a birthday, a best hockey game, swimming lessons, a trip to the hospital, trouble with a pet, a time with grandparents, a funny experience, or an embarrassing time.

Together with a partner, have the students share a little about each of their listed topics and choose one to write about. Then suggest that they ask each other questions about the chosen topics to help the authors make some decisions on what to include in their writing. To model this questioning technique,

Explain to the students that the topics they choose should be about something that they actually experienced and that they were part of, rather than writing about a topic they only heard about. In this way, they will be able to make their writing about the memory more personal.

have students ask you questions on a topic you have chosen to write about, write them on the board, and discuss if and how the answers to these questions would make your writing more interesting and complete.

Encourage students to record the questions they are asked in their journals so they can refer to them while writing. Suggest that they also "question" their topics themselves to help them decide what should go into their writings. When they are satisfied with the questions they need to answer in their writing, they can write a first draft on their topic.

Topic — My favorite party
Questions
– How old were you?
– What was the occasion?
– Where was the party?
– Who was at the party?
– What was the best part of the party?
– Why was this your favorite party?

 Assessment See **Assess Learning**, page 23.

Visual Communication

Design a Collage

Discuss with students what a collage is and jot their ideas on the board or on chart paper. Have the students design a personal collage of their favorite season. Suggest that they plan the collage first by jotting how they feel about the season, what they enjoy doing most, and any other ideas about the season they would like to get across, and then listing what materials they could use for each of their ideas.

When the collages are complete, have pairs of students exchange their collages and, on an index card, provide feedback on them. The feedback should be based on the criteria the students established in the beginning. For example:

Did the collage
– tell a main idea or message?
– use materials of different sizes and shapes?
– use a variety of materials such as photos, fabric, and paper?
– have the different pieces overlapping or touching?

After reading the feedback, have the students add a note about what they would do differently the next time they composed a collage. Also, have them indicate what they felt they did well. Have the students save their cards for future reference.

A Collage

- has a main idea or message
- uses materials of different sizes and shapes
- uses different kinds of materials (pictures, paper, fabric, foil, …)
- can have words, sentences, numbers, and symbols
- can have own drawings
- the pieces of a collage are glued on cardboard or paper
- the pieces overlap or touch each other

LINK TO CURRICULUM

Language Arts

Create a Season Poetry Book

The students could work together to create an anthology of season poems organized around the four seasons. They could select poems of their own and ones they find in anthologies or other sources. Ask them to copy down the author and source of the poem so this information can be put with the poems.

The poems could be copied using a word processing program and illustrated with a graphics program or with freehand drawings. (See pages 5 and (ii) for more information.) Bind the poems into a class poetry book for the classroom or the school library.

Create a Guessing Game

Pairs of students could construct a game box. Using a box about the size of a shoebox, have them cut a hole in the lid that would allow a hand to fit through. Then they put an object inside the box, secure the lid, and ask classmates to see if they can guess what is in the box by touch only. The "trick" for the game makers is to choose objects that could fool the players.

Encourage the students who are guessing to describe what the object feels like before they guess. Suggest that a number of students try their hand at guessing each object before its identity is revealed. In this way, students can compare their experiences with the sense of touch.

Science

Research Seasonal Changes

Students could carry out research about what causes particular seasonal changes. One source of information would be an encyclopedia CD-ROM. (See pages 5 and (ii) for more information.) To lead the investigation, they could brainstorm a number of questions they would like to answer.

Then pairs of students could choose one question to answer. The students could come together and share their answers orally, using pictorial aids to help with their explanations.

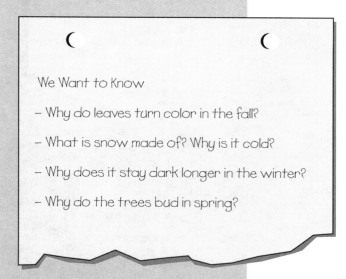

We Want to Know

– Why do leaves turn color in the fall?

– What is snow made of? Why is it cold?

– Why does it stay dark longer in the winter?

– Why do the trees bud in spring?

Social Studies/Science

Compare Seasons

Have pairs or individual students choose two seasons, and using a Venn diagram, compare them from several perspectives such as
- clothing
- special foods
- weather conditions
- outdoor games
- outdoor colors

Students who have lived in other parts of the country or in other countries, or who know someone who has lived in another country that they can interview, might like to do a Venn diagram comparing the same season in two different places. Have the students share their diagrams.

Assess Learning

Assessment

Writing (see p. 20)

For **individual assessment** of students, ask them to select those questions that they used to guide their personal writing.
Look for evidence that the student has
- chosen guiding questions appropriate to their topic.
- used the guiding questions to help shape their writing.
- an understanding that guiding questions can assist them as writers.

Use this opportunity to conference individually with a few students to praise their use of guiding questions to support the writing or to coach those who might benefit from help in looking at examples where guiding questions were used to support writing.

Moments and Memories

In this selection, children share stories about memories that have special significance to them. The stories are personal and reflect each writer's true voice.

Anthology, pages 12-15

Learning Choices

LINK TO EXPERIENCE

Share Photographs

Reflect on Memories

READ AND RESPOND TO TEXT

READING FOCUS
- make judgements and draw conclusions about the content in written materials, using evidence from the materials
- STRATEGY: **read and reflect**

REVISIT THE TEXT

mini LESSONS

READING
Share Personal Interpretations

Assessment

- explain their interpretation of a written work, supporting it with evidence from the work and from their own knowledge and experience

WRITING
Keep a Writing Log
- communicate ideas and information for a variety of purposes and to specific audiences

ORAL COMMUNICATION
Tell a Story

Assessment

- communicate a main idea about a topic and describe a sequence of events

LINK TO CURRICULUM

LANGUAGE ARTS
Write an Anecdote

LANGUAGE ARTS/THE ARTS
Make a Thank You Card

THE ARTS
Role-Play a Scene

MATHEMATICS
Tally Information

Key Learning Expectations

Students will
- make judgements and draw conclusions about the content in written materials, using evidence from the materials **(Reading Focus, p. 25)**
- explain their interpretation of a written work, supporting it with evidence from the work and from their own knowledge and experience **(Reading Mini Lesson, p. 26)**
- communicate ideas and information for a variety of purposes and to specific audiences **(Writing Mini Lesson, p. 27)**
- communicate a main idea about a topic and describe a sequence of events **(Oral Communication Mini Lesson, p. 27)**

LINK TO EXPERIENCE

Share Photographs

Invite students to bring in personal photographs about a special time they spent with family or friends. Bring some of your own in to share with them. Show a photo and talk about the experience it depicts, telling why it is special for you.

Then, in groups, have students do the same with their photographs. Students who do not have photos to share could draw a picture to share or simply tell about a favorite memory.

Reflect on Memories

Discuss with students what memories are and why we remember certain things more vividly than others. They might suggest that we remember things that evoked strong emotions, such as happiness, surprise, fear, embarrassment, and sadness.

Ask students to jot in their journals strong personal memories they have and categorize them according to the emotions they felt at the time. Some students might like to share their memory categories with a classmate.

Happiness
– holiday to the mountains with my family
– winning the Little League pennant
Surprise
– getting my puppy
– getting an A in Math
Fear
– getting lost my first Hallowe'en
– watching X-Files with my brother

READ AND RESPOND TO TEXT

Reading Focus

Using a **read and reflect** strategy, read the first narrative with the students or have them read it independently. Ask them to share with a partner what they learned about the child who wrote the story. List a volunteer pair's responses. Then ask them to tell why they think these things are true, using proofs or ideas from the narrative.

Get Ready to Read

Tell the students that the selection will feature children's stories about special personal memories. Ask them to predict what they think the children might have written about. Record their ideas on the board for checking against following the reading of the selection.

What We Learned about Sean

- He likes his dad.
- He has a sense of humor.
- He's ten years old.
- He's a good storyteller because of the way he writes. He uses a lot of talking in his story.
- He likes to have fun.
- He has lots of friends.

Have the students read the remaining stories either independently or with a partner, and summarize in their journals what they learned about each author from the narratives. They can share their summaries with another classmate, explaining their choices.

Reader Response

Students could
- illustrate one of the children's stories.
- write a letter to one of the authors, telling what they enjoyed most about the story.
- in small groups, share their own stories about moments and memories similar to those they read about in the selection.
- choose a favorite story and explain why it is a favored narration, using a pattern of cause and effect.

I like the story written by Naomi because she realized something special about her brother that she didn't know before and that was great.

Reading

Share Personal Interpretations

Invite the students to think about their personal interpretation of the story written by Naomi—how they feel about the story, what they learned from it, and what was the main theme of this particular narration. Have them jot their interpretations in a two-column organizer.

Use a conversation circle approach to have the students share their initial interpretations with one another. For conversation circle sharing,
- arrange students in circle groups and divide each circle of students in half using a rope or chalk line.
- for each group, the students in one semi-circle listen attentively while those in the other semi-circle take turns telling about their interpretations.
- place a "talking chip" in one semi-circle; when students are ready to share, they take the chip and speak in turn.
- once all the students in the semi-circle have had a turn, those in the other semi-circle summarize what they learned from the speakers.
- then the students in the semi-circles switch roles.

Following the conversations, invite the students to consider the opinions of their classmates and write their new interpretations in the after-sharing column of the organizer. Some students may find that they do not wish to change their writing, and others may find that, after hearing other points of view, they now feel differently.

A "talking chip" can be any object — a pen, a block, a counter, a custom-designed disc,... — that is picked up by someone in a group who wishes to speak, and replaced within reach of others when he or she is finished speaking.

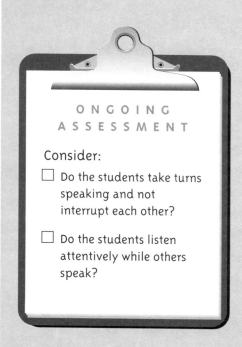

ONGOING ASSESSMENT

Consider:
- ☐ Do the students take turns speaking and not interrupt each other?
- ☐ Do the students listen attentively while others speak?

Interpretation before Sharing	Interpretation after Sharing
The story was about a boy finding a lost cat his home.	Now I think the story was about doing the right thing, no matter how hard it is.
I liked the story because it had a lot of good description.	My classmates thought that Naomi learned a lot about her brother from what he did. I never thought of that.
I learned that if you keep trying, things will work out okay.	

Writing

Keep a Writing Log

Have the students look through the narrations in the selection and list the various topics that the children wrote about. Discuss possible reasons why the authors chose them.

Talk with the students about the choices, pointing out that
- the authors' story ideas came from experiences that involved them personally.
- the experiences were very meaningful to the authors.
- the stories involved people who were close to them.

Invite the students to think of and record three or four topics they could write about. The topics should reflect the three points of criteria you discussed.

Explain that it is sometimes difficult to recall topics in detail. Suggest that jotting down ideas, words, phrases, places, people, and so on about a possible writing topic will help them when they decide to write about the topic.

Have the students reserve a space in their personal journal to keep a log of topics and details from which they could select and shape their written memories and moments. Then ask them to select one of their topics and jot details about it that they would like to remember for future writing.

accident at recess
- blood, bad cut on forehead, crying
- everyone helped the little boy
- teacher came to see what happened

friends
- funny, make me laugh
- Lisa is my best friend
- she can do super cartwheels

birthday party
- sunny
- went swimming
- diving in deep end
- Jesse nearly drowned

Oral Communication

Tell a Story

Discuss with the students good tips for storytelling. Record these on chart paper.

Ask students to choose one of the stories from the selection or one of their own "moments and memories" stories to tell. Suggest that they
– jot the main points of the story they want to cover.
– decide on details they want to include (can elaborate on those in the selection and add new ones).
– practise telling their story to a partner.

When they are ready, the students can tell their story to a group of classmates.

Storytelling Tips
1. Choose a story you know well. If it's a new story, read it over and over.
2. Plan what you want to say using notes.
3. Practise telling your story before telling it to an audience.
4. Make the story interesting by
   – using a lot of expression in your voice
   – using facial expressions to show feelings
   – using gestures that match what is happening in the story
   – using props or sound effects if you wish
4. Look at the audience while you tell the story.

Assessment

See **Assess Learning**, see page 29.

LINK TO CURRICULUM

Language Arts

Write an Anecdote

Have the students write about a personal memory. They could choose a topic that they have already thought about or started planning. They could revise their stories on computer, and then share their stories with other classmates by displaying them on a bulletin board, reading them to others, or compiling them into a class book.

Using a software program such as *Creative Writer 2*, students could transform their stories into slide shows, which could be stored on diskette in the computer centre. (See pages 5 and (ii) for more information.)

Language Arts/The Arts

Make a Thank You Card

Students could make a thank you card that one of the writers of the selection might send to the person(s) responsible for giving them the special memory or moment. Suggest that the students look at commercial thank you cards before designing their own.

On the front of the cards, they could draw pictures or find magazine pictures to cut and paste that are related to the story, or they might prefer to create a more commercial design. Encourage them to write a message on the inside that describes why they are sending the card—why the moment was special. Students could display the cards and share and compare them.

The Arts

Role-Play a Scene

Students could work in groups or pairs to role-play a scene from one of the stories from the selection. For example, they could work in a group to dramatize Sean's birthday party or the Thanksgiving dinner at Keshia's, or in pairs to show what happened when Avi returned the cat.

Encourage the students to plan what is going to happen, supplying their own details where necessary, and to practise the scene, improvising the dialogue. They can then share their scenes with each other.

Mathematics

Tally Information

Groups of students could survey their classmates and ask them to rate the stories from the selection from 1 to 6, with 1 being their favorite. Suggest they design a survey sheet to give to each student to record their opinions. Once the opinions have been recorded, discuss with the students how they could determine how the class as a whole rated the stories and how they could record this information in a tally chart.

Have the students share their tally chart once they have consolidated the information.

Selections						
	Sean	Keshia	Chengyin	Benito	Naomi	Nyla
Roberto	3	1	6	5	4	2
Maelynn	1	6	3	5	2	4
Kirstin	1	5	2	4	3	6
Nestor						

Assess Learning

Oral Communication (see p. 27)

(see p. 27)

Within each group, have students **peer-assess** each storyteller. Establish criteria for the assessment from the "Tips" chart developed by the students. Each item could be rated on a scale from 1 to 5, with 5 being the highest. Students should be given an overall rating as well.

Or students could use the *Assessing Storytelling* Assessment Master from the *Assessment Handbook*.

Note: You may wish to tape-record the students so they can do a self-assessment after.

The students could include the assessment sheets in their portfolio of work samples. Have individual conferences with selected students to look at the assessments and talk about successes as well as areas for improvement.

Assessing Storytelling

Name of Storyteller _____ Date: _____

Rate the storytelling on a scale of 1 to 5, with 5 being the highest.

Knowledge of the story

The storyteller:
• appears to have practised the story	1	2	3	4	5
• knows the story really well	1	2	3	4	5
• has a good beginning that makes you want to listen	1	2	3	4	5
• has a good ending	1	2	3	4	5

Ability to make the story interesting

The storyteller:
• puts a lot of expression into the voice	1	2	3	4	5
• uses facial expression to show feelings	1	2	3	4	5
• uses gestures that match the action of the story	1	2	3	4	5

Qualities of Speaking

The storyteller:
• speaks loudly enough	1	2	3	4	5
• speaks slowly enough	1	2	3	4	5
• looks at the audience	1	2	3	4	5
• appears to be relaxed	1	2	3	4	5

Something I think the storyteller did well is _____

A suggestion I have for the storyteller is _____

_____
Assessor's Signature

COLLECTIONS Copyright © 1997, Prentice Hall Ginn Canada.
Permission to reproduce this page is restricted to the purchasing school.   **Assessment Master (Student) 61**

How I Got My Dogsled

In this picture book, the sister team of Jackie Lewis and Cindy Crew write and illustrate a story of a caring young girl who befriends a stray dog, and, with her friend, trains the dog and two of her pups to wear a harness and pull a sled.

Anthology, pages 16-21 Blackline Master 22 Learning Strategy Card 5

Learning Choices

LINK TO EXPERIENCE

Brainstorm About Dogsleds

View Books or Pictures About Working Dogs

READ AND RESPOND TO TEXT

READING FOCUS
- explain their interpretation of a written work, supporting it with evidence from the work and from their own knowledge and experience [Assessment]
- STRATEGY: **read and reflect**

REVISIT THE TEXT [mini LESSONS]

READING
Respond to Different Types of Questions [Assessment]
- make judgements and draw conclusions about the content in written materials, using evidence from the materials

WRITING [Assessment]
Write "How To" Instructions
- use writing for various purposes and in a range of contexts
Language Workshop — Spelling
- hard/soft g;/ŭ/sound

VISUAL COMMUNICATION
Read a Double Image Picture
- identify the main characteristics of some media

LINK TO CURRICULUM

LANGUAGE ARTS
Discuss Responsibilities as a Pet Owner

SOCIAL STUDIES
Find Out About Community Garbage

THE ARTS
Illustrate a Part of the Story

SCIENCE
Research Sled Dogs

Key Learning Expectations

Students will
- explain their interpretation of a written work, supporting it with evidence from the work and from their own knowledge and experience (**Reading Focus, p. 31**)
- make judgements and draw conclusions about the content in written materials, using evidence from the materials (**Reading Mini Lesson, p. 32**)
- use writing for various purposes and in a range of contexts (**Writing Mini Lesson, p. 33**)
- identify the main characteristics of some media (**Visual Communication Mini Lesson p. 34**)

LINK TO EXPERIENCE

Brainstorm About Dogsleds

Show the students a picture of a dogsled and ask them to brainstorm what they know about dogsleds and what they can tell from the picture. Jot their responses on the board or overhead transparency. Then have them categorize and web the information.

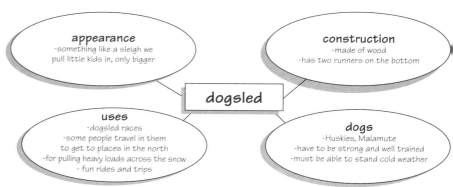

appearance
-something like a sleigh we pull little kids in, only bigger

construction
-made of wood
-has two runners on the bottom

dogsled

uses
-dogsled races
-some people travel in them to get to places in the north
-for pulling heavy loads across the snow
- fun rides and trips

dogs
-Huskies, Malamute
-have to be strong and well trained
-must be able to stand cold weather

View Books or Pictures About Working Dogs

Invite students to talk about different ways dogs and humans can work together. Have them look through books, pictures, and other resources about working dogs to find and share information. Have them note what breeds are often used for particular jobs.

Students may wish to make pictures with descriptive sentences about the various types of dogs and their work to post in the classroom.

READ AND RESPOND TO TEXT

Reading Focus

Use a **read and reflect** strategy. The students can read the story one page at a time, stopping at the end of each page to jot down at least one important event that took place.

Following their reading, students can work in small groups to list the important events in sequence and discuss how they think the characters felt in each one. With the whole group, compile a consolidated list of events in sequence on a chart, with notes about the characters' feelings.

EVENTS	CHARACTERS' FEELINGS
- the stray Husky has pups in the hound's doghouse	- the pup's mother might have felt proud and tired - the hound was probably mad because the Husky was in his doghouse
- the storyteller and her mom go to see the dogs and find out they will probably be shot	- they would be upset and unhappy because they didn't want to see the dogs die
- the storyteller and her mom bring the dogs home	- they would be happy and relieved because the dogs wouldn't be killed

Reader Response

Students could
• share experiences of their own or those from a book or movie that they were reminded of when reading this story.
• in a small group, role-play the conversation that might have gone on when the girls were trying to convince their parents to let them each keep one of the pups.
• retell a favorite part of the story orally or in writing.
• read the trade book version of the story with the complete set of illustrations.

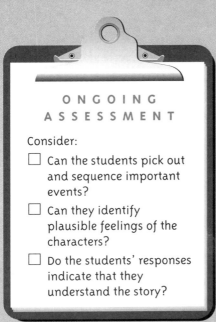

Get Ready to Read

Read the first two paragraphs of the story with the students. Discuss what this introduction tells them about the story line, the setting, and the characters.

ONGOING ASSESSMENT

Consider:
☐ Can the students pick out and sequence important events?
☐ Can they identify plausible feelings of the characters?
☐ Do the students' responses indicate that they understand the story?

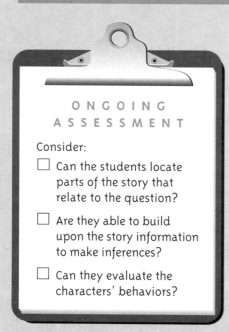

ONGOING
ASSESSMENT

Consider:

☐ Can the students locate parts of the story that relate to the question?

☐ Are they able to build upon the story information to make inferences?

☐ Can they evaluate the characters' behaviors?

R EVISIT THE TEXT

Reading

Respond to Different Types of Questions

Learning Strategy Card 5

To help students to define and identify literal, inferential, and evaluative questions, make use of Learning Strategy Card 5, *Types of Questions*. You might want them to do practice activities on the card, and/or have them locate and read aloud answers as found in the text (designated by the page number), and then expand their thinking when asked. Use questions such as the following:

Literal ("in the story")
• What are you told about the stray dog that just had puppies? (page 17)
• What things did the storyteller do for the dogs when they returned from a dogsled trip? (page 21)

Inferential ("in my thoughts")
• What is said about the hound dog's behavior that gives you an idea about how he is feeling? (page 17) How do you think he happened to be out in the cold?
• What did Uncle Paul tell the girls to be sure to teach their dogs? (page 21) What do you think would happen if the dogs chased rabbits?

Evaluative ("in my judgement")
• What did the neighbor say he might have to do with the stray dog that had just had puppies? (page 17) Why would he say that? What do you think about his idea?
• What was the storyteller's reply when the kids wanted rides on the sled? (page 21) What did you think of the way the situation was handled? What would you have done and why?

Students can work with a partner to write a literal, inferential, and evaluative question for this story or another one they have read in the anthology. The questions can be written on strips of paper and exchanged with another group.

Writing

Write "How To" Instructions

Ask students to locate and reread the parts of the story telling how the two girls trained their dogs to pull a sled. With the whole group, discuss what the girls did and make a list of the steps in sequence. Talk about how to write these steps as a set of instructions for others to follow, bringing out points such as

- use short sentences
- use words that clearly explain what the person is to do
- start sentences with action words
- go step-by-step
- give the steps in the right order, using signal words such as "first," "next," "then," "after," and so on.

Together, write a set of instructions for training a sled dog. Include a section describing what things the girls needed for the training and another section at the end describing special tips for training. The instructions could be written on chart paper under three headings: What You Need, What You Do, and Special Tips.

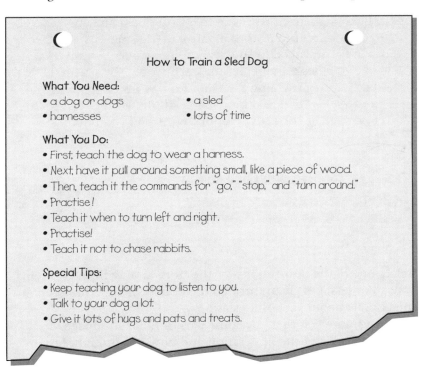

How to Train a Sled Dog

What You Need:
- a dog or dogs
- harnesses
- a sled
- lots of time

What You Do:
- First, teach the dog to wear a harness.
- Next, have it pull around something small, like a piece of wood.
- Then, teach it the commands for "go," "stop," and "turn around."
- Practise!
- Teach it when to turn left and right.
- Practise!
- Teach it not to chase rabbits.

Special Tips:
- Keep teaching your dog to listen to you.
- Talk to your dog a lot.
- Give it lots of hugs and pats and treats.

Students can then each write their own set of "how to" instructions for doing something they are familiar with, and later compile them into a *How To Do Many Things* manual. They might use computer software to create and/or embellish the instructions and the manual. (See pages 5 and (ii) for more information.)

 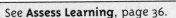 See **Assess Learning**, page 36.

HOW I GOT MY DOGSLED

• hard/soft g; /u/ sound patterns

village	strange	shovel
hungry	guided	minute
drugged	guess	enough
garbage	investigate	smother

Theme/Challenge Words

• art words

landscape	mural	portrait
collage	fresco	

Early Words

• compound words

firewood	someone	upset
doghouse	dogsled	

Blackline Master 22   • hard/soft g; /ŭ/ sound

Explore and Discover

Use Blackline Master 22 and the **sort**, **share**, **discuss**, and **chart** procedure outlined on page 16 to work with the words.

In discussing the words, have students note the vowels that follow the hard and soft "g" sound, and the different vowels that make the "short u" sound. Draw their attention also to the final consonant that has been doubled in "drugged" and review the reason why.

Follow this exploration with a **pretest**, **study and practise**, and a **post test** as outlined on page 16.

Study and Practise

Students could
• use Learning Strategy Card 3 to study words identified after the pretest.
• arrange their word cards in alphabetical order, going to the third letter for some of them. They can then copy the alphabetized words onto a strip of paper.
• play a riddle game with a partner. The students give five words they need to study to their partners, who think of two clues to help identify each word. The partners take turns providing the clues for a word to be guessed and spelled by the other person. If the word is guessed and spelled correctly, that player receives a point.

Visual Communication

Read a Double Image Picture

Select one of the illustrations for the story and, with the students, consider messages given through the double or superimposed image. Talk about such things as:
• how a frame is formed by some part of the front image.
• the main idea of the illustration and how it is brought out.
• what supporting information is given.
• clues provided by the illustration about the cultural background and lifestyle of the characters.
• how the illustration enhances the message of the text.
• what they like or dislike about the illustration.

Together, summarize the points brought out in the discussion under four selected headings, using a piece of paper to make a Four-Fold Commentary sheet.

Have students select another illustration and make a Four-Fold Commentary. Those who have commented on the same picture can gather in a group and discuss their completed commentaries, noting similarities and differences in their ideas.

Main Idea
- it's in the heart-shaped frame that's in front
- the mother wants to take good care of the puppies

Supporting Details
- she has a nice soft blanket and a box for a bed for the puppies
- maybe the sun and trees and things are the decorations on the blanket

About the Characters and Setting
- I think she's Native because that's what the art around the picture of her looks like

What I Think
- I like the picture, but I wish I could see if the blanket was all bright colors

LINK TO CURRICULUM

Language Arts

Discuss Responsibilities as a Pet Owner

In small groups, students can discuss topics related to the responsibilities of pet owners, such as
- the kinds of things that have to be done to look after a pet's needs.
- things pets do that annoy other people in the family, neighbors.
- what can be done to keep pets from bothering others.
- what could/should happen if people do not look after their pets properly.

One person in the group can be designated to take notes during the discussion. Using these notes as a guide, students can plan how to share their thoughts with the larger group.

Social Studies

Find Out About Community Garbage

Recall the garbage dump in the story, and invite students to discuss how their community, town, or city disposes of garbage and what it does to limit the amount of garbage. They might like to invite a guest speaker to the classroom who could provide more information about sanitary disposal in their area.

Students might also like to come up with a list of ways that they can reduce, reuse, and recycle in the classroom to cut down on the amount of garbage that gets "thrown away." They could also talk to their families about what they do personally to limit the amount of garbage in their homes and, if necessary, decide on actions they could take to improve the situation.

 Some students might like to present information they have gathered in a brochure or poster made using computer software. (See pages 5 and (ii) for more information.) Completed posters could be displayed around the school to encourage environmental awareness.

The Arts

Illustrate a Part of the Story

Invite students to think back on the story and choose a part they could illustrate, using a style similar to that of Cindy Crew in the selection. When their illustrations are completed, students could ask a classmate to peer-assess their pictures using a Four-Fold Commentary format.

Science

Research Sled Dogs

 Discuss what information the students got about sled dogs from the story and what they know from prior knowledge. Ask students to suggest sources of further information about sled dogs and activities with dogsleds. Elicit such possibilities as books, CD-ROMs, the Internet, videos, pamphlets from winter carnivals that have dogsled races, and dogsled tour brochures. (See pages 5 and (ii) for more information on computer resources.)

Students can list questions they would still like answered about sled dogs and check various resources to find the answers. The answers could be written in a report or shared orally with the whole group in a discussion.

Assessment A s s e s s   L e a r n i n g

Thinking About the Instructions

Name of writer _____

Did the writer:	YES	NO
• use short sentences?	☐	☐
• use words that clearly explain what the person is to do?	☐	☐
• start each sentence with an action word?	☐	☐
• go step-by-step?	☐	☐
• give the steps ain the right order?	☐	☐
• add other sections to the instructions?	☐	☐

What I likes most about the instuctions was _____

_____

_____

The part of the instructions that made the most sense was _____

_____

_____

What I find difficult to understand _____

_____

_____

Suggestions I have _____

_____

_____

_____

Writing (see p. 33)

Arrange students in pairs to **peer-assess** their "How To" instructions. They can read and/or listen to each other's instructions, and use the points from the activity as a guide for their assessment, along with some questions. After completing the assessment forms, the partners can talk with one another about ways to make improvements.

Don't Just Sit There, Get a Hobby

In this humorous story by Mary Wood, Uncle Phil, who is always telling Ken what to do, gets a big surprise when he urges Ken to find himself a new hobby.

Anthology, pages 22-27   Blackline Masters 4 and 23

Learning Choices

LINK TO EXPERIENCE

Tell About a Humorous Experience

Identify Favorite Hobbies

READ AND RESPOND TO TEXT

READING FOCUS
- read a variety of fiction and non-fiction materials for different purposes
- STRATEGY: **guided reading**

REVIST THE TEXT

READING
Describe a Character
- make judgements and draw conclusions about the content in written materials, using evidence from the materials

WRITING
Language Workshop — Punctuation
- use correctly the convention of punctuation (speaker tags in dialogue)
Language Workshop — Spelling
- two-syllable words; soft c

ORAL COMMUNICATION
Interview and Introduce a Classmate
- use appropriate words and structures in discussions or classroom presentations

LINK TO CURRICULUM

LANGUAGE ARTS
Share a Joke

THE ARTS
Create a Comic Strip

SCIENCE
Make a Fact Sheet About Snakes

Find Out About Canning

Key Learning Expectations

Students will
- read a variety of fiction and non-fiction materials for different purposes **(Reading Focus, p. 38)**
- make judgements and draw conclusions about the content in written materials, using evidence from the materials **(Reading Mini Lesson, p. 38)**
- use correctly the convention of punctuation (speaker tags in dialogue) **(Writing Mini Lesson, p. 39)**
- use appropriate words and structures in discussions or classroom presentations **(Oral Communication Mini Lesson, p. 40)**

LINK TO EXPERIENCE

Tell About a Humorous Experience

Arrange the students in sharing circles to tell about a time when something funny happened to them or someone close to them. Explain that their experience should be one that makes them laugh when they think about it. You might wish to share a funny experience of yours first.

After the sharing, discuss with the whole group those things that the students thought were the funny elements in the stories.

Identify Favorite Hobbies

Discuss what a hobby is. Then give each student a piece of paper and ask them to write what their favorite hobby is. Have a volunteer collect and read the hobbies aloud as you record and tally them on the board.

Ask the students to group the listed hobbies in categories: team sports, individual sports, the arts, and so on. Then ask them if they can make any generalizations about the favorite hobbies of the class.

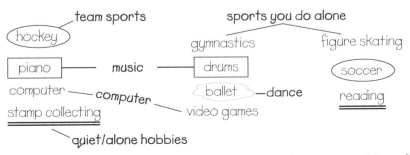

Get Ready to Read

Read the synopsis to the students and then have them scan the illustrations to predict what new hobby Ken chooses for himself.

Reading Focus

Using a **guided reading** strategy, read aloud or have the students read independently to the end of "I'll be back later."(page 24). Ask students to talk about the humor in the section: what they found funny and why. Then have them predict what will happen next.

Follow the same procedure, stopping at

- *Together we got the new snake into a fourth jar.* (page 25)
- *So we hurried back to my house to pick up the snake jars.* (page 26)
- the end of the story

Students could jot funny phrases, dialogue, descriptions, …, from the story in their journals.

Reader Response

Students could
- hold a conversation about the story, using questions such as:
  - **What do you think is the most humorous part of the story? Why?**
  - **What did the author do in her writing that made this a humorous story?**
  - **Does this author's writing remind you of another author you've read? Who?**
  - **Although this is a funny story, do you think the author was trying to make a point? What might it be?**
  - **Does anything in the story remind you of something that has happened to you or someone you know?**
- role-play their favorite scene from the story.
- write captions for the illustrations in the story.
- write a personal response to Ken's feelings towards grown-ups: *You can't please them no matter how hard you try.*

 See **Assess Learning**, page 42.

REVISIT THE TEXT

Reading

Describe a Character

Ask the students to describe Uncle Phil. They might say that he is in good shape, thinks he knows everything, is not too old, maybe in this twenties, has a girlfriend, and so on. Have them find and share proofs for their ideas from the story.

About Uncle Phil

In good shape:
He began to ripple his muscles.
His arms bulged.
Uncle Phil got down on the floor and did a few push-ups.
"Look at me. A strong body built from regular exercise is a joy to behold."

Building on the proofs the students find in the story, elicit the following generalizations: readers learn about a character from
– what the author says about the character.
– what the character says (dialogue).
– what the character does (action).
– what other characters say.

Invite the students to choose another character from this story or one from another story they have read and make a list of things they know about the character and the proofs for what they know. Remind them to look for examples from the four categories discussed. They could share lists with a partner.

Writing

Language Workshop — Punctuation

Blackline Master 4

Have students revisit the story to find dialogue and note the variety of speaker tags the author uses. They might notice words such as "asked," "snapped," "answered," "interrupted," and "hollered." Then ask them to look closely at the dialogue to see where the author placed the speaker tags in the sentence, noting that she
– put speaker tags at the beginning of the dialogue
– in the middle of dialogue
– at the end of dialogue

> Speaker tags are verbs that describe how dialogue is spoken.

Students may also note that there are places where no speaker tags are used at all.

At the same time, have them look closely at the placement of punctuation — especially quotation marks — for the different placements of the speaker tags.

Using examples from the story, review and generalize the rules regarding the placement of quotation marks and other punctuation and the use of capitals.

Have the students complete Blackline Master 4, *Writing Dialogue*, to practise using quotation marks and using a variety of speaker tags in different placements.

Interested students could use picture tools on software such as *Creative Writer 2* to draw Uncle Phil or another character. This would help them focus on the details. (See pages 5 and (ii) for more information.)

Blackline Master 4

DON'T JUST SIT THERE, GET A HOBBY

- two-syllable words; soft "c" pattern

problems	complaints	pieces
voices	subject	advice
couple	trouble	teaches
disgust	relax	twice

Theme/Challenge Words

- hobby words

recreation	pastime	relaxation
diversion	pursuit	

Early Words

- high utility words (irregular spellings)

build	built	only
easy	sure	

You may want to first talk about what constitutes a "hobby" and brainstorm some examples.
If some children have no hobbies, the interview could be revised to focus on favorite foods or animals.

Language Workshop — Spelling

- two-syllable words; soft c

Blackline Master 23

Explore and Discover

Use Blackline Master 23 and the **sort**, **share**, **discuss**, and **chart** procedure outlined on page 16 to work with the words.

Have students clap out the syllables in the words and talk about how they think the words would be divided into syllables. Together, note the words that have two syllables and which of these have a common syllable— "es," " __le." They can refer back to the list for "A Morning to Polish and Keep" or their wall chart for other words with the "__le" pattern.

List the soft "c" words on a chart that can be added to over time. Note the vowel that follows the "c," making it a soft sound, and brainstorm words with this and other influencing vowels.

Follow this exploration with a **pretest**, **study and practise**, and a **post test** as outlined on page 16.

Study and Practise

Students could

- use Learning Strategy Card 3 to study words identified after the pretest.
- mark the syllabic divisions for the words on their cards, spelling the words aloud softly as they do.
- make a grid of words with a common letter in each word. For example, students make a vowel row on a piece of paper and fit spelling words into the row.

```
problEms
subjEct
  tEaches
advicE
rElax
```

Oral Communication

Interview and Introduce a Classmate

Have the students work in pairs to interview each other about their favorite hobby. Before the interview, discuss what kinds of questions the interviewer might ask to get the information needed and develop a form they could use in the interview.

Interview Questions

Name: _____

Hobby: _____

How did you get interested in this hobby?_____

How long have you been doing it? _____

Why do you like it? _____

What have you learned from it? _____

Would you recommend this hobby to your friends? Why? _____

After the interviews, have students "introduce" the person they interviewed to the class by orally presenting the information they got during the interview. Beforehand, have students discuss ways they can make their introductions effective; for example,
– using all the information gathered.
– organizing it in a way that will make sense to the listener.
– speaking clearly.
– using appropriate tone of voice.

Encourage the students to practise their introductions before presenting them to the class.

LINK TO CURRICULUM

Language Arts

Share a Joke

Have the students locate and research joke books and choose several of their favorites to share aloud to a classmate. Remind them that in order to successfully tell a funny joke to an audience they should remember that
– the joke should not make anyone feel uncomfortable.
– the joke should be memorized.
– it should be at the interest level of the audience.
– it should be told with good expression.

When the students feel confident, invite them to tell and share their funny jokes to a number of small groups of classmates.

The Arts

Create a Comic Strip

Imitating the artistic style of the illustrations in the story, the students can create an eight frame comic strip. The comic strip could feature another humorous adventure for Kenneth and Uncle Phil, or students could use the ideas from a personal funny story of their own for the comic strip.

They could include the dialogue of the comic characters. Display the comic strips for everyone to enjoy.

Interested students could use a software program to draw a comic strip, then add speech balloons and text. They could then transform their comic strips into slide shows and store them on diskettes. (See pages 5 and (ii) for more information.)

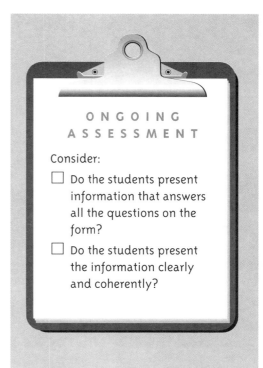

ONGOING ASSESSMENT

Consider:

☐ Do the students present information that answers all the questions on the form?

☐ Do the students present the information clearly and coherently?

Science

Make a Fact Sheet About Snakes

With a partner, students can locate information about snakes by looking through a variety of resources and prepare a fact sheet that includes things Kenneth would need to know to take care of them. Recall that fact sheets give important information in a short, concise way, usually with the aid of headings. They could concentrate on one kind of snake or on snakes in general. Suggest that they illustrate their fact sheet and display it for others to read.

Find Out About Canning

Students could interview a family member or neighbor who does canning to find out what they can and how they do it. They could share the results of the interview with classmates orally or in a short report. Or they could write directions for canning something that they like.

Alternatively, students might like to find out about the reasons behind different canning processes, either in the home or in industrial plants—what needs to take place in canning different foods so they are safe to eat—and share the information with their classmates.

Assessment

A s s e s s   L e a r n i n g

Reader Response (see p. 38)

Reader Response Activity Sheet

Date: *October 12*   Name: *Mama*
Reading Selection: *Don't Just Sit There, Get a Hobby*

Activity I chose to do:
I wrote captions for the illustrations.

Why I chose it:
I wanted to write something funny.

How I think I did on it:

How my teacher thinks I did on it:

Plan time to assess the response activity that the students chose. To prepare for the assessment, students could complete a **self-assessment** using the *Reader Response Activity Sheet* from the *COLLECTIONS Assessment Handbook*.

OR

You might prefer to have the students write answers to the questions in "hold a conversation" about the story. Use the written answers as a **work sample** assignment or as a test of how well they comprehend the story.

Place the students' answers and your marks in their portfolios.

Note: With some students, you may prefer to hold individual conferences so that they can answer orally.

THEME:
SPECIAL MOMENTS AND MEMORIES

Anthology, pages 28–29

Family Reunion — *a memoir*

Whipping Cream — *anecdotes*

Camp-Out Disaster — *a poem*

LINK TO THE THEME

After reading the selections, students could

- prepare three questions (literal, inferential, and evaluative) to ask each other about moments or memories in any of the selections.
- read aloud to a partner a selection that reminds them of an experience of their own, and tell about the similarities.

LINK TO THE WRITING PROCESS

Write a Memory Poem

Ask students to think of a special moment or memory of their own. Have them use paper strips to jot words or phrases that come to mind as they recall the experience. To help plan their poems, they can move the paper strips to try different orders and arrangements. They can write a free verse poem or a rhyming four-line stanza patterned after "Camp-Out Disaster."

Language Workshop — Style

- use correctly the conventions of punctuation (parentheses)

Blackline Master 5

Teach/Explore/Discover

Draw students' attention to the author's use of parentheses in the selection "Family Reunion" and in the part he wrote about himself. Have volunteers read aloud the sentences with parentheses, or in the case of the whole sentence in parentheses, that sentence and the one immediately before it. Together, talk about how the author used parentheses, noting that the parts in parentheses add information that is not necessary to the story, but is interesting, and in this case, also add humor. Tell them that phrases or sentences in parentheses are often referred to as "asides." Ask students to read the sentences again, this time paying attention to how they might read the parts in parentheses to show that they are asides.

Have students find another example of parentheses in "Whipping Cream." Then together, look at stanzas one to four in "Camp-Out Disaster" to find lines that could be put in parentheses because they provide additional information (asides).

- Our class went on a camping trip. (And, boy, what a mistake.)
- Next was horseback riding. (At that I was no ace.)

Practise/Apply

Students could

- complete *Adding Information*, Blackline Master 5.
- find other places in "Camp-Out Disaster" where parentheses could be put around parts that add information.

Blackline Master 5

LINK TO THE WRITER

Have students read what Jared says about the kinds of stories he likes to write, and talk with a partner about questions such as the following:

- Why do you think the author finds it easier to write horror and adventure stories?
- Do you share the author's point of view? Why or why not?
- What kinds of stories do you like to write? What atmosphere would help you to write that kind of story?

STUDENT WRITING

Shelter Folks

Virginia Kroll writes a touching story in which a young girl first feels the humiliation of having to move into a shelter, but as time goes on, she becomes proud to call the people in the shelter "my folks."

Anthology, pages 30-39   Learning Strategy Card 6
Blackline Masters 6 and 23

Learning Choices

LINK TO EXPERIENCE

Discuss the Title

Chart Different Types of Homes

READ AND RESPOND TO TEXT

READING FOCUS
- explain their interpretation of a written work, supporting it with evidence from the work and from their own knowledge and experience **Assessment**
- STRATEGY: **read, pause, and reflect**

REVISIT THE TEXT

mini LESSONS

READING
Appreciate and Interpret Idioms
- understand the vocabulary and language structures

WRITING
Write a Personal Narrative **Assessment**
- produce pieces of writing using narrative techniques
Language Workshop — Spelling
- compound and multisyllabic words

VISUAL COMMUNICATION
Symbolize Important Parts of Your Life
- create a variety of media works

LINK TO CURRICULUM

LANGUAGE ARTS
Write About a Character

THE ARTS
Illustrate Figures of Speech and Idioms

SOCIAL STUDIES
Research Community Shelters or Special Homes

MATHEMATICS
Plan a Budget

Key Learning Expectations

Students will
- explain their interpretation of a written work, supporting it with evidence from the work and from their own knowledge and experience **(Reading Focus, p. 45)**
- understand the vocabulary and language structures **(Reading Mini Lesson, p. 45)**
- produce pieces of writing using narrative techniques **(Writing Mini Lesson, p. 46)**
- create a variety of media works **(Visual Communication Mini Lesson, p. 48)**

LINK TO EXPERIENCE

Discuss the Title

Invite the students to discuss what is meant by the term "shelter folks." They could first look up the word "shelter" in the dictionary, and then consider how its meaning might be applied to the title of the story. Talk about the different things people might need shelter from, and how we help provide that shelter in our communities.

Chart Different Types of Homes

In small groups, students can brainstorm different types of homes and talk about the advantages of each of them. They can then plan and make an illustrated and labelled chart showing the various types of homes. The charts can be displayed for other groups to look at.

Kind of Housing	Description	Picture
Single family house	- a house not attached to another house - can be one, two, or even three stories	
Duplex	- a house divided into two separate houses - can be up and down or side-by-side	
Row houses		

READ AND RESPOND TO TEXT

Reading Focus

Blackline Master 6

 Students can use a **read, pause, and reflect** strategy to consider various events and reflect on different characters' thoughts and points of view. Some may choose to listen to the *COLLECTIONS 5* audio version. The pause points and questions on Blackline Master 6, *Read and Reflect,* can be used to guide their reading and discussion with a partner or group.

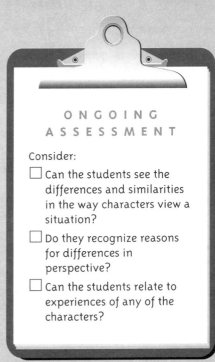

Blackline Master 6

Reader Response

Students could
- write three questions to ask another student about the story — a literal, inferential, and evaluative question.
- draw a favorite part of the story and write a caption for the picture.
- dramatize the conversation that might have gone on between Joelle and Nathaniel about her moving, if the bell had not rung just at that moment. Or role-play the scene that might have happened after the Thanksgiving play ended.
- list possible reasons why Joelle and Eli felt differently about moving to the shelter, and consider which one of the two they might be more like.
- make a list of characteristics they think are important in a friend.

 # REVISIT THE TEXT

Reading

Appreciate and Interpret Idioms

With the students, talk about how authors sometimes use words and phrases that help readers form pictures in their minds so they can understand characters, places, and ideas better. Have students locate some examples in the story. Write these on strips of paper or use an overhead transparency. ▶

Get Ready to Read

Read aloud to students the conversation between Joelle and her brother Eli at the beginning of the story. Tell them that this dialogue introduces a problem that underlies the story in "Shelter Folks." Ask them to predict what the conversation is about and what will follow. They can check their predictions as they read on in the story.

ONGOING ASSESSMENT

Consider:
- ☐ Can the students see the differences and similarities in the way characters view a situation?
- ☐ Do they recognize reasons for differences in perspective?
- ☐ Can the students relate to experiences of any of the characters?

Idioms are descriptive expressions. Their meaning cannot be taken literally from that of the individual words. For example, I have caught a cold; I was so mad I nearly exploded.

Figures of speech also cannot be taken literally. They are picturesque descriptions that build comparisons and help you see something in a new way.

Descriptive phrases also help enhance meaning through imagery, but in a more literal way.

Explain what an idiom is, and ask students to select the strips with idiomatic expressions. Use appropriate examples to assist them in seeing how idioms differ from figures of speech and descriptive phrases. Then ask them to look through the story for more idioms and record these.

Talk about the meaning of these idioms, and ask students to paraphrase their meanings in their own words. Discuss how idioms enhance the story. These idioms can be recorded for display and added to as the students find others in their reading or conversations.

IDIOMS

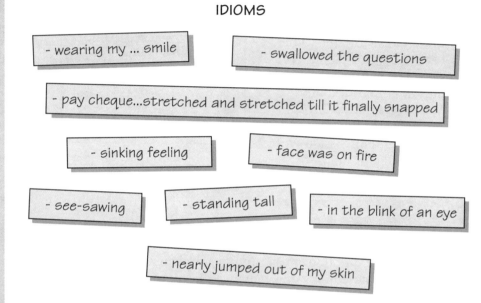

- wearing my ... smile
- swallowed the questions
- pay cheque...stretched and stretched till it finally snapped
- sinking feeling
- face was on fire
- see-sawing
- standing tall
- in the blink of an eye
- nearly jumped out of my skin

Writing

Write a Personal Narrative

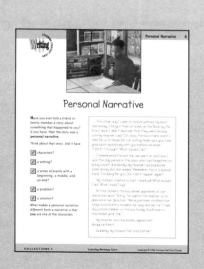

Personal Narrative

Learning Strategy Card 6

Explain to the students that, although this selection is a story, if it were true, it would also be a personal narrative. This is because it is the experience of a person as told by the person that it happened to. With this in mind, refer to Learning Strategy Card 6, *Personal Narrative*, and discuss with the students the structure and language of the story, pointing out that
– it has an interesting beginning and ending.
– the events are told in sequence.
– the author explains where the story happens.
– the author explains who all the characters are.
– the author uses good description.
– the author explains how the main character feels.

Using the suggested activity on the Learning Strategy Card, expand the students' ideas about the selection into a writing plan they can follow for their own personal stories.

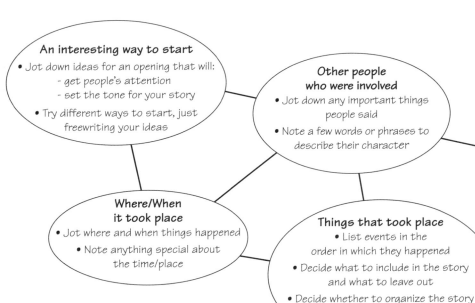

An interesting way to start
- Jot down ideas for an opening that will:
  - get people's attention
  - set the tone for your story
- Try different ways to start, just freewriting your ideas

Other people who were involved
- Jot down any important things people said
- Note a few words or phrases to describe their character

Words to describe how I felt during the experience
- List as many words as you can

Where/When it took place
- Jot where and when things happened
- Note anything special about the time/place

Things that took place
- List events in the order in which they happened
- Decide what to include in the story and what to leave out
- Decide whether to organize the story by time, importance of events, or some other way

The way things ended
- Jot down ways to end your story:
  - tell how you felt about your experience
  - tell how it might affect what you do in the future
  - end with a thought or question

Students can then plan and write a personal narrative, telling of an experience of their own when they felt proud about something. After they have completed their first draft, have them check their writing for capitalization, punctuation, and spelling, and refer to their writing plan to see if they missed anything or could do something a little better.

The stories can be compiled into a booklet for the classroom library. The authors could also tape a reading of their stories so others can listen and follow along.

A personal narrative is a non-fiction story, so both narratives and stories involve the same steps in writing.

 Assessment See **Assess Learning**, page 50.

SHELTER FOLKS

- compound and multisyllabic words

apartment	blueberry
yesterday	sandwiches
elevator	piano
sweatshirt	recognize
breakdown	actually
neighborhood	(neighbourhood)
countertop	

Theme/Challenge Words

- drama words

characters	rehearsing
rehearsal	performance
narrator	

Early Words

- /are/pattern

fare	care	share
share	sharing	

 A related homework project is to make a "special times" mobile. See *Home Connections Newsletter*, Blackline Master 2.

Language Workshop — Spelling

Blackline Master 23   • multisyllabic words; compound words

Explore and Discover

Use Blackline Master 23 and the **sort**, **share**, **discuss**, and **chart** procedure outlined on page 16 to work with the words.

Students can first divide the compound words into their word parts, and then clap out the words to make further syllabic divisions. In pairs, they can clap out the syllables for the other words and talk with each other about where they think the divisions would come. Bring out words that have irregular spellings, and discuss with students ways to remember them.

Follow this exploration with a **pretest**, **study and practise**, and a **post test** as outlined on page 16.

Study and Practise

Students could

- use Learning Strategy Card 3 to study words identified after the pretest.
- work in pairs to look up their words in a dictionary and write each word in its syllable parts on the back of the word cards.

a part ment	coun ter top	el e va tor	pi an o

- write humorous sentences using two or three spelling words in each sentence and underlining the words.

Visual Communication

Symbolize Important Parts of Your Life

Read aloud the lines from the selection, "We filled the other one with my books, my two dolls, my hair fasteners, my dinosaurs. My whole life." Ask students to recall what those lines are referring to and discuss how Joelle's various belongings probably represented parts of her life that were important to her. Invite students to talk about things that could represent important aspects of their lives, explaining the connections.

Brainstorm with students how they might represent their lives using these things as "symbols" of what is important to them. They might suggest using pictures, drawings, and other representations of these real things in a collage, a scrapbook, a treasure box, or a crest. Students can then each choose and create a way to represent their lives. These representations can be displayed, and each student can give an oral presentation to explain the meaning behind each of the symbols.

LINK TO CURRICULUM

Language Arts

Write About a Character

In pairs, students can choose a character from the story, brainstorm words they would use to describe that character, and talk about things from the story that tie in with the traits they've identified (actions, descriptions, conversations, …, that exemplify or prove a trait). Individually, they can write a short paragraph about the character, read their character descriptions to one another, and make suggestions for improvement.

Some students might like to first draw their chosen character using software with picture tools. (See pages 5 and (ii) for more information.)

The Arts

Illustrate Figures of Speech and Idioms

Recall the figures of speech identified when looking for language in the story that helped form images in the reader's mind. Invite students to select a few of the figures of speech to illustrate. In small groups, students can then talk about their illustrations, talk about how the figures of speech helped them to understand the characters, places, or ideas, and compare their interpretations.

> They [plastic trash bags] flew across the room and lay there **like shiny rectangular snakes.**

> But I gave him **dagger eyes,** and he clammed up.

> Mama shook out a trash bag. The flat snake turned into a **huge round balloon.**

> Outside the wind swept the leaves **into a circle dance.** They whirled **like all the feelings swirling in my chest.**

> They just stared, **statue-still,** with wide-open eyes and wider-open mouths.

For fun, students might like to make cartoon illustrations for such idioms as
– I've caught your cold.
– She drives me up the wall.
– It's raining cats and dogs.
– Don't count your chickens before they hatch.
– My cousin is really sharp.

Students could display their illustrations and organize a "Guess the Idiom" contest.

Social Studies

Research Community Shelters or Special Homes

In small groups, students can work together to gather information about different kinds of shelters or special homes in their community. They might start by listing shelters they know about and then going to other sources, such as the yellow pages in the phone book, social service agencies, a community map, churches, the Internet, and so on, for other names.

Students can consider different ways to gather information about these places, such as writing for information or talking to someone who works there. Once the information has been gathered, they can decide what to do with their information. They may want to write reports, compile a community shelter/special home booklet, or plan and carry out a project that would assist those in the shelter or home.

Mathematics

Plan a Budget

Have students imagine that they receive $5.00 for a weekly allowance. Ask them to plan a budget for spending this money, including saving any for a special project, if they wish. Tell them that they have to provide for anything extra that they might want during a week (not including meals or snacks that their parents or the school provide or other real necessities).

 Once the budgets are complete, have students take them home to share with their families and talk about how realistic they are, particularly in terms of how much things cost. Students can then make any necessary revisions based on the discussions.

Assessment

A s s e s s   L e a r n i n g

I remembered to check for:
- ☐ spelling
- ☐ periods, question and exclamation marks, quotation marks
- ☐ capital letters for beginnings of sentences, names, and so on
- ☐ descriptive words
- ☐ an interesting beginning
- ☐ a good ending

Something I think I did well is _____
_____

Something I need to do better is_____
_____

Writing (see p. 47)

After completing their story and its revisions, students can fill out a **self-assessment** sheet. Their planning charts, final drafts, and self-assessment sheet can used as **work samples**. You might wish to assess the writing too, using the same points as in the self-assessment.

OFFERINGS

These free verse poems, written by Janet Wong, offer reflections on two relationships between a child and an older person, with both involving learning and teaching.

Anthology, pages 40-41   Learning Strategy Cards 7 and 8
Blackline Masters 7 and 8

Learning Choices

LINK TO EXPERIENCE

Listen to a Story

Talk About Traditions

READ AND RESPOND TO TEXT

READING FOCUS
Assessment
• read a variety of fiction and non-fiction materials for different purposes
• STRATEGY: **listen and read along**

REVISIT THE TEXT

READING
Compare the Poems
Assessment
• explain their interpretation of a written work, supporting it with evidence from the work and from their own knowledge and experience

WRITING
Write a Diamante Poem
• produce pieces of writing using a variety of forms

ORAL COMMUNICATION
Choral Read in Two Parts
• use tone of voice, gestures, and other non-verbal cues to help clarify meaning when reading aloud

LINK TO CURRICULUM

LANGUAGE ARTS
Write a Free Verse Poem

SOCIAL STUDIES
Brainstorm Ways to Help

THE ARTS
Create a Special Card

MATHEMATICS
Graph Living Arrangements for Seniors

Key Learning Expectations

Students will
• read a variety of fiction and non-fiction materials for different purposes **(Reading Focus, p. 52)**
• explain their interpretation of a written work, supporting it with evidence from the work and from their own knowledge and experience **(Reading Mini Lesson, p. 52)**
• produce pieces of writing using a variety of forms **(Writing Mini Lesson, p. 53)**
• use tone of voice, gestures, and other non-verbal cues to help clarify meaning when reading aloud **(Oral Communication Mini Lesson, p. 54)**

LINK TO EXPERIENCE

Listen to a Story

Read aloud a short story, chapter from a novel, or a picture book about a relationship between a younger and older person. Ask students to talk about the relationship: what the two thought of one another, did together, learned from one another, and how they cared for one another. Then invite them to write in their journals about a relationship of their own or others they know about that this selection reminded them of. They can exchange journals with a partner and read each other's entries.

BOOKS ABOUT YOUNG/OLD RELATIONSHIPS

Thunder Cake. Patricia Polacco. Philomel Books, 1990.
Grandpa's Garden Lunch. Judith Caseley. Greenwillow, 1990.
The Auction. Jan Andrews. Douglas & MacIntryre, 1990.
Just Like Max. Karen Ackerman. Borzoi, 1990.
The Outside Child. Nina Bawden. Lothrop, Lee and Shepard, 1991.
When I Am Old With You. Angela Johnson. Orchard, 1990.

Talk About Traditions

Ask students to share information about traditions that have been passed down in their families, such as ways of celebrating special occasions, ways of dressing, cultural dances, a craft or skill, special recipe, and so on. Jot their responses on the board or chart paper.

Then in pairs or small groups, students can describe the tradition, tell how it gets passed on to other family members, tell why they think the tradition is or is not important, and suggest whether or not they will continue it when they grow up.

Get Ready to Read

Write the titles of the two poems on the board and ask students to brainstorm what they think each of them is about.

ONGOING ASSESSMENT

Consider:

☐ Do the students understand the main idea of each poem?

☐ Can they describe the relationship between the younger and older characters in each poem?

In making **comparisons**, you tell how things are alike and how they are different. In **contrasting** things, you only tell how they are different.

READ AND RESPOND TO TEXT

Reading Focus

Using a **listen and read along** strategy, read one poem aloud at a time, while students follow along in their books. After each reading, have students talk about the poem and identify the main idea of the poem.

In pairs, they can discuss the learning/teaching relationship between the younger and older characters in the poem, and brainstorm words that describe the characters and how they felt about one another. To conclude, have each pair paraphrase the main message of each poem and share what they have written with other pairs.

Reader Response

Students could
- choose the poem they like better and tell a partner why it appeals to them more than the other poem.
- draw an illustration to accompany one of the poems.
- write in their journal about a personal experience, book, or movie that one of these poems brought to mind.
- choose a book, story, or poem to read to another person, perhaps someone who is sick, or elderly, or who cannot see well, or a young child.

REVISIT THE TEXT

Reading

Compare the Poems

Talk with the students about similarities and differences they noticed in the two poems. In the discussion, help them to consider such things as style of writing, main message, characters and their relationships, events, general tone, ….,. Together, organize the points from the discussion into a comparison chart, similar to the one shown.

Have students choose two books, stories, or poems they have read and make a comparison chart for them, then share and explain their chart with a partner.

SIMILARITIES	DIFFERENCES	
"Lucky" and "Tea Ceremony"	"Lucky"	"Tea Ceremony"
– both are about people	– about a neighbor and a friend	– about a grandfather, mother, and child
– both have younger and older characters	– tells about John Lee who isn't there	– the grandfather and mother are there
– both tell about learning and teaching	– the child reads to John Lee	– the child pours tea for the grandfather
– both are free verse poems	– has only one verse	– has three verses
– both are by the same author	– John Lee probably wasn't trying to teach the child, just enjoyed reading with her	– mother is teaching child how to do something exactly
	– the child likes John Lee as a friend	– the child respects her grandfather

Assessment See **Assess Learning**, page 56.

Writing

Write a Diamante Poem

Learning Strategy Card 7

Remind the students that both poems are free verse: they don't follow a specific pattern. Suggest that they write about the ideas in the poems using a different kind of poem, a diamante poem.

Explain that a diamante poem is a seven-line poem that contrasts two ideas and has the following pattern:

Line 1: One word that is the title
Line 2: Two words that describe the title
Line 3: Three words that are actions of the title
Line 4: Four words: two words are things about the title;
      next two words are things about the opposite
Line 5: Three words that are actions of the opposite
Line 6: Two words that describe the opposite
Line 7: One word that is the opposite of the title

Work together to compose a diamante that builds on ideas expressed in one of the poems. You may also want to use words and phrases from the original poem, along with others that fit in with the poem's ideas.

> Audience
> focused, polite
> listens, watches, imagines
> ears, eyes, voice, lips
> whispers, shouts, pauses
> expressive, smooth
> reader

Students can write their own diamante about the other poem, about something they've done or would like to do with an older family member or friend, or about any topic they wish. Learning Strategy Card 7 can be used as a reference and for activity ideas for writing diamantes.

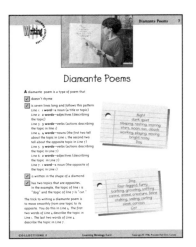

DIAMANTE POETRY

A **diamante** contrasts two ideas. It starts with one idea and details about that idea. Halfway through it changes to details about the opposite of the idea. It ends with the opposite. Diamantes are written in a diamond shape.

Oral Communication

Choral Read in Two Parts

Learning Strategy Card 8

Have the students reread one of the poems silently to consider such things as:

• the mood of the poem. Is it humorous? thoughtful? tense? happy?

• appropriate pause and stopping points. Where would you pause or stop to make sure that the ideas in the poem flow as one unit?

• parts where they can use voice or gestures to enhance the meaning. What words or phrases might be spoken softly/loudly? Should some parts be read more quickly than others? Are there any places where hand or body gestures would fit?

> In a two-part choral reading, two or more voices alternate reading verses, sentences, or other sections of text.

Invite a few students to read the poem aloud, keeping in mind the above considerations. Have other students listen and comment on the mood, flow, and expression, as well as clarity of speech and the pace of the readings.

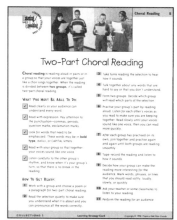

In small groups, have students practise two-part readings of either poem, dividing the poem into alternating pieces any way they wish. They might like to use Learning Strategy Card 8, *Two-Part Choral Reading*, to help them plan and practise. Have students share their choral reading with the whole group.

LINK TO CURRICULUM

Language Arts

Write a Free Verse Poem

Using a free verse form, students can write a poem telling about a ceremony they have seen or been part of. They might write about the opening ceremonies at the Olympic Games or at a hockey game, a graduation or awards ceremony, a wedding, ….,.

> In free verse, there is no set rhyme pattern, no set rhythm, and no set line lengths.

Students can compile a book of these poems. They might like to make the book "expandable" so that other poems they write can be added. In this way, their poetry book can have different sections or parts of poems based on different topics or forms.

Social Studies

Brainstorm Ways to Help

Talk with students about how in "Lucky," the teaching, learning, and doing roles became reversed as John Lee grew older. In small groups, students can brainstorm activities they can do together with a senior or older person and ways in which they can help an older person. They should also brainstorm things that older people might be able to teach them. If possible, they should talk to older people to get their input. Each group can record their ideas in a web or chart to be shared later with the whole group.

Activities together	Learn from them	Help them
– play Scrabble	– how to knit	– using a computer
– go to a show	– how to play Hearts	– read the newspaper to them
– go for a walk	– about my relatives	– run errands

As a class, you might want to choose a seniors' residence, nursing home, or community centre that has senior programs, and develop a plan whereby students may become buddies with seniors on an ongoing basis.

The Arts

Create a Special Card

Blackline Masters 7 and 8

Students can follow the instructions on Blackline Masters 7 and 8, *Make a Pop-up Card*, to create an open-arms pop-out card to give to an older person on a special occasion. They can write inside the card a personal message that is appropriate for the occasion.

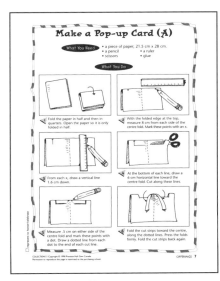

Blackline Master 7

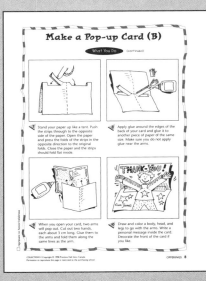

Blackline Master 8

Mathematics

Graph Living Arrangements for Seniors

Ask students to tell about the living arrangements (whether they live on their own and in what type of housing) of seniors they know: family, friends, or neighbors. List these on the board as they are given. Put those who live on their own or with a spouse in one column, and those who live with others (children, in a group) in another. Then, in each column, tally the number who live in similar residences: single dwelling house, duplex, apartment, condominium, basement suite, trailer, seniors' residence, nursing home, and so on.

Have pairs of students organize and depict the information in two graphs, one for each column. When the graphs are finished, ask them if they can make any generalizations about a connection between seniors living on their own or not and the type of housing they live in.

Assessment

Assess Learning

Reading (see p. 52)

Use selected students' charts as **work samples** to assess their ability to make comparisons. Talk with each of the students about the differences and similarities between the two poems, stories, or books they have chosen. Students thinking at a higher level will often talk about the differences in a parallel way. For example, if they were comparing the two poems in the selection, they would say that in "Tea Ceremony," the child pours tea for the grandfather, and in "Lucky," the child reads to John Lee.

The author of the poems "Lucky" and "Tea Ceremony," Janet S. Wong, is an accomplished presenter at conferences, workshops, and assemblies. To enquire about her school (student) packages or teacher inservice package, contact:

  Anne Mao Moss, Publicist
  Simon & Schuster
  Children's Publishing Division
  1230 Avenue of the Americas
  New York, NY 10020
  (212) 698-2805

Helping Hands

This article tells about a group of young people who, when they were in grade 5, started a club to help people. They have embarked on a number of helping projects that have provided challenges, fun, and friendship.

Anthology, pages 42-45   Learning Strategy Card 9
Blackline Masters 9, 10, and 24

Learning Choices

LINK TO EXPERIENCE

List Ways of Helping Others

Gather Books About Clubs

READ AND RESPOND TO TEXT

READING FOCUS
• explain their interpretation of a written work, supporting it with evidence from their own knowledge and experience
• STRATEGY: **read and connect**

REVISIT THE TEXT

READING
Outline the Article
• read a variety of fiction and non-fiction materials for different purposes

Assessment

WRITING
Write a Note to Parents
• communicate ideas and information for a variety of purposes and to specific audiences
Language Workshop — Spelling
• multisyllabic words; ness, y patterns

ORAL COMMUNICATION
Plan Guidelines for Listening
• listen and respond constructively to the ideas of others when working in a group

Assessment

LINK TO CURRICULUM

LANGUAGE ARTS
Write a Diary Entry

SOCIAL STUDIES
Learn About an Organization

THE ARTS
Make a Friendship Bracelet

Prepare a Dramatization

SCIENCE
Make an Environmental Awareness Flyer

Key Learning Expectations

Students will
• explain their interpretation of a written work, supporting it with evidence from their own knowledge and experience (**Reading Focus, p. 58**)
• read a variety of fiction and non-fiction materials for different purposes (**Reading Mini Lesson, p. 59**)
• communicate ideas and information for a variety of purposes and to specific audiences (**Writing Mini Lesson, p. 60**)
• listen and respond constructively to the ideas of others when working in a group (**Oral Communication Mini Lesson, p. 61**)

LINK TO EXPERIENCE

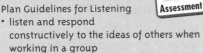
List Ways of Helping Others

Have students think of things that they can do to help others. Write their ideas on the board. Ask the students to work in groups to categorize the ideas according to criteria of their own choosing; for example, types of jobs, ages of people being helped, errands, entertainment or fun, …,. They could add other ideas they think of as they are categorizing. As a whole group, share the categories.

The students can note in their journals ideas from the list that they have already done or jot ways they can think of to help someone they know.

Gather Books About Clubs

Ask students to recall books they have read or heard about that are stories about clubs formed by or for children their age. Encourage them to bring such books from home and the library to display. Provide opportunities for the students to tell something about the books they've gathered and to recommend some of their favorites to classmates.

BOOKS ABOUT CLUBS
Author-of-the-Month Club.
Sheila Greenwald. Little, Brown, 1990.
Baby-Sitters Club series.
Ann M. Martin.
The Basement Baseball Club.
Jeffrey Kelly. Houghton Mifflin, 1987.
Eco Kids series. Kathryn Makris.
The Green Musketeer series.
Sara St. Antoine.
Henry and the Clubhouse.
Beverly Cleary. Morrow, 1962.
Saddle Club series. Bonnie Bryant.

READ AND RESPOND TO TEXT

Get Ready to Read

Introduce the selection by having students look at the picture on the first page and read the information in the introductory paragraph on page 42 to find out who the Helping Hands are and to get an idea of what the article is about.

Use Blackline Master 9, *Listening Behaviors/Skills*, to record first-time observations of a student(s) in one of the conversation circles. A second observation can be recorded following the Listening/Speaking mini lesson on page 61.

Listening Behaviors/Skills

Student _____ Date _____

Listening Behaviors/Skills	1st	2nd	Comments/Improvements
The Listener: • looks at the speaker	☐	☐	
• stays still, doesn't fiddle or squirm	☐	☐	
• shows signs of interest: nods, smiles,...	☐	☐	
• doesn't interrupt	☐	☐	
• asks appropriate questions after the speaker finishes	☐	☐	
• makes appropriate comments after the speaker finishes	☐	☐	
• makes comments/questions that show that he/she remembered what was said	☐	☐	
• makes comments/questions that are related to what the speaker said	☐	☐	

COLLECTIONS 5 Copyright © 1998 Prentice Hall Ginn Canada.
Permission to reproduce this page is restricted to the purchasing school.   HELPING HANDS 9

Blackline Master 9

Reading Focus

Use a **read and connect** strategy. To start, ask volunteers to read aloud the diary entries and notes that are placed around the club photo. After each reading, invite students to comment on the activity and share personal experiences that come to mind.

Then have students read through the article silently on their own and make jot notes about a helping experience of their own or others that they thought of as they read. They can then gather in conversation circles to share their thoughts. (See page 26 of this book, "Moments and Memories," for information on conversation circles.)

As a whole group, students can share their jot notes. Or they can compare the ways of helping in the article and their personal experiences with the list they made earlier.

Reader Response

Students could:
• hold a conversation about the story with a partner or in a group to discuss questions such as:
  – **What reasons do you think Angie had for starting the Helping Hands Club?**
  – **Why would making phone calls be the hardest part for most of the members?**
  – **How could making the boy in the hospital smile be part of his recovery?**
  – **How might the girls have known that the people in the seniors' home enjoyed their program, even though they "didn't cheer much"?**
  – **Which one of the club activities would you be most interested in doing and why?**
• read books about clubs from the classroom display or from the library.
• think of a way they could help out in their community and plan a telephone conversation to that place or person offering their services.
• write about a worthy cause they would like to raise money for and brainstorm ways of doing it.

REVISIT THE TEXT

Reading

Outline the Article

Learning Strategy Card 9

Model the process and format of creating an outline of an existing piece of writing by
• using Learning Strategy Card 9.
• working with the selection.

Ask students to identify the two sections of the article and write these as main headings in an outline on the board or an overhead transparency. Have them reread the article and jot down words or phrases that give the main ideas of each of the sections. Jot these as subheadings. Then ask them to find or recall important details of each subhead and write them under the related subheading.

Together look over the outline that has been written to determine if it correctly summarizes the information in the article and if the points are in the appropriate order. Make changes where necessary.

A Club with a Cause

Forming the club
- for helping people
- volunteer work
- logo and friendship bracelets

Club Members
- changed sometimes
- take projects seriously
- became close friends
- have fun
- learn how to do things

A Parade of Projects

Environmental month
- cleaned up
- passed out flyers

The SPCA
- too young to walk dogs
- fundraising instead

Little kids' baseball team
- practices and games

You might wish to show students how to use letters and numbers in an outline or any other method you prefer that shows the hierarchy of the ideas.

Students can use this approach and refer to Learning Strategy Card 9 to outline and summarize another article, perhaps from a curriculum area such as social studies or science, or to organize information for a research project.

 See **Assess Learning**, page 62.

Main headings identify the most important kinds of information in the whole article. They mark the sections of an article.

Subheadings identify the main ideas in each section of the article.

Details or **sideheads** identify important points or examples for each main idea in a section.

ONGOING ASSESSMENT

Consider:

☐ Can the students distinguish between main ideas and details (subheads and sideheads)?

☐ Can the students arrange information sequentially as it was presented in the article?

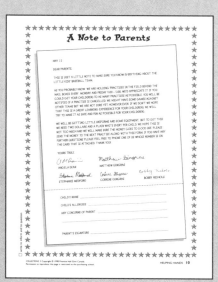

Blackline Master 10

Suggest that students keep their notes for possible use or reference if they plan community activities later on.

HELPING HANDS

• multisyllabic words; ness, y patterns

donation	version	recovery
willingness	awareness	library
security	shyness	nursery
completion	diary	business

Theme/Challenge Words

• volunteer words

volunteering	donations
commitment	organization
contribution	

Early Words

• "ar" pattern

| parks | hard | backyard |
| started | part | |

Writing

Write a Note to Parents

Blackline Master 10

Make an overhead transparency of Blackline Master 10, *A Note to Parents*, written by the Helping Hands. Have the students read the note silently and pick out important information that is provided in the body of the letter. List this information on the board.

Ask students what other information they might like to have if they were the parents. They can also suggest changes to the wording and make these additions or changes on the overhead. Go over the note again, looking at the type used and the paragraphing. Discuss and make any changes.

Then look at the tear-off strip. Discuss why this information from parents would be necessary, and ask students to suggest other information that might be asked for in a tear-off information sheet.

In pairs or individually, students can select an activity they would like to organize for young children and write a note for it that includes an information tear-off sheet.

Language Workshop — Spelling

Blackline Master 24   • multisyllabic words; ness, y patterns

Explore and Discover

Use Blackline Master 24 and the **sort**, **share**, **discuss**, and **chart** procedure outlined on page 16 to work with the words.

Have students choose five of the more difficult words. Write these on the board or overhead, and with the students, clap out the syllables and focus on spelling the words by syllable. Note how "ness" and "y" are separate syllables. Also, in the discussion, talk about the differences between the pronunciation and formation of "business" and the other words with the "ness" pattern.

Follow this exploration with a **pretest**, **study and practise**, and a **post test** as outlined on page 16.

Study and Practise

Students could

• use Learning Strategy Card 3 to study words identified after the pretest.

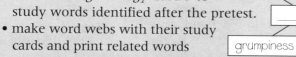

• make word webs with their study cards and print related words or words with the same patterns on blank cards and add them to the web.

• play a tic-tac-toe game with a partner. The players make a fairly large nine-square game grid and, in turn, use a different colored marker to write a study word in a square. The object is for one player to write three words in a vertical, horizontal, or diagonal line.

Oral Communication

Plan Guidelines for Listening

Refer to the club members' visits to the Good Samaritan nursing home. Discuss what things they might have talked about with the seniors and what difficulties they might have encountered in their conversations. Elicit that the children would probably have to be very good and patient listeners in this situation. Use this idea to bring out the importance of being attentive and caring listeners in all conversations.

Good Listening Guidelines

1. Show that you are listening
   - look at the person
   - stay still without fiddling with things
   - show signs of interest when appropriate
     – nod
     – smile
     – look concerned if the speaker is

2. Pay attention to what the person is saying
   - think about things to remember
   - think of questions to ask later

3. Don't interrupt

Have the students brainstorm things that would be important to keep in mind when listening. Together, draw up some guidelines for listening.

Arrange students in groups to choose a topic and hold a discussion, keeping in mind the guidelines for good listeners.

LINK TO CURRICULUM

Language Arts

Write a Diary Entry

Have students look again at the club diary entries on the first page of the article and together note features that are included: date, place, who, specific details about what happened, reflection. Ask students to recall something of significance to them and write about it in their journals as a diary entry, using the club diary entries as a guide.

Social Studies

Learn About an Organization

Students can work in small groups to gather information about a non-profit, helping organization in their community, such as an animal care group (SPCA, Humane Society, PAWS, …). They could write for informational brochures on the organization, visit the organization to conduct an interview, or talk to people who have been helped by the organization. Together, they can decide how to present their information effectively to the class.

In drawing up the listening guidelines, students can think back to their experiences in the conversation circle.

ONGOING ASSESSMENT

Use Blackline Master 9 again to compare listening behaviors of students in the conversation circle in the Reading Focus activity with those shown in the discussion groups here. For ease of assessment, students should work in the same groups for both activities.

Consider inviting members of service clubs and organizations in the community to visit the classroom, speak to the students, and answer questions.

The Arts

Make a Friendship Bracelet

Students can make a friendship bracelet like the ones club members made in the selection. Someone who knows how could help a group of students make them, or students could follow the instructions in a craft book such as *Friendship Bracelets* by Camilla Gryski. Students can make the bracelets for themselves or to exchange with a friend.

Prepare a Dramatization

The Helping Hands chose *Little Red Riding Hood* as the play to perform for the seniors because they wanted a story that many of the people would remember from their childhood. Invite students to work in small groups to prepare a drama of a familiar story that they could present to seniors. After practising, they can put on the play for seniors or perhaps for younger classes in the school.

Science

Make an Environmental Awareness Flyer

When the Helping Hands created Environment Month, they passed out flyers with suggestions for ways people in their neighborhood could care for the environment. Groups of students can plan a flyer telling about environmental concerns in their neighborhood and giving suggestions for what can be done to make a difference.

Students could then share their plans and come up with one flyer plan. The flyer could be published, copied, and passed out to their neighbors.

 There are software programs geared to the production of flyers and other printed material. (See pages 5 and(ii) for more information.)

 Assessment

A s s e s s   L e a r n i n g

Reading (see p. 59)

Have the students include their outlines as a **work sample** in their portfolios. Hold individual conferences to assess how they were able to use outlines to organize information. Look for the ability to:
• identify main ideas as headings
• record supporting details for each main idea
• review the outline and identify interesting or useful information.

 Students could work on friendship bracelets at home as a home connection project. See the *Home Connections Newsletter*, Blackline Master 2.

Working Out Problems — *a poem*

Dear Mrs. Hicks — *a letter*

Talk with Me — *a poem*

LINK TO THE THEME

After reading the selections independently or with a partner, the students could

• write a few sentences about each selection, telling how each is related to the theme of people helping each other.

• draw a picture or series of pictures telling about an experience of their own that came to mind when reading one of the selections.

LINK TO THE WRITING PROCESS

Write a Thank You Letter

Blackline Master 11

Make an overhead transparency of Justin's letter to Mrs. Hicks. Work with the students to pick out features of this thank you letter and label them on the transparency. Discuss the purpose of each of the features. Note that a date, return address, and closing are missing from Justin's letter. Explain that most letters would include these. Show on the transparency where these would go.

Together, talk about what needs to be included on the envelope and develop criteria for correctly addressing an envelope, including the sender's return address.

Make an ongoing chart listing things/people they could write thank you letters to, and display commercial thank you cards for ideas.

Then have students write and address a thank you letter, using *All-In-One Thank You Letter*, Blackline Master 11. Suggest that they write their letter before cutting it out.

Language Workshop — Style

• use conventions of various media (typeface in text)

Blackline Master 12

Teach/Explore/Discover

Use the poem "Talk with Me" to demonstrate how to use typeface to emphasize a thought, pattern of thinking, or action, and/or to convey an emotion. Reread the poem with the students and discuss with them why they think the writer capitalized certain words in the poem, and how this assists them as readers.

Look back at the poem, "That Was Summer," on pages 10 and 11 of this anthology. Have the students read this poem silently and suggest how capitalized words could have been used.

You may also wish to work with examples of poems or stories in which italics or boldface type have been used for emphasis.

Practise/Apply

Students could

• complete Blackline Master 12, *Words in Capitals.*

• look through other poems and stories to find places where capitalized words have been used to emphasize thoughts or actions, or to convey emotions.

LINK TO THE WRITER

Recall how Laura wanted to write a book like *Goosebumps.* Invite students to talk in small groups about their favorite books and why these books are their favorites. Have each group record a list of their favorite books on a chart and include the author and student name for each. Post the charts so students can refer to them when looking for a book.

 Students may want to look for their favorite stories on software. (See pages 5 and (ii) for more information.)

STUDENT WRITING

Hot Wheels!

This article introduces the Mini Lights basketball team, a team made up of young, physically disabled kids who wheel around the basketball court in practice drills and pickup games.

Anthology, pages 47–49   Blackline Masters 13, 14, and 24
Learning Strategy Card 10

Learning Choices

LINK TO EXPERIENCE

Talk About Being in a Wheelchair

Experience Basketball

READ AND RESPOND TO TEXT

READING FOCUS
• explain their interpretation of a written work, supporting it with evidence from the work and from their own knowledge and experience

Assessment

• STRATEGY: **read and paraphrase**

REVISIT THE TEXT

mini LESSONS

READING
Read a Newspaper Article
• read a variety of fiction and non-fiction materials for different purposes

WRITING
Write an Article with Headings
• produce pieces of writing using a variety of forms
Language Workshop — Spelling
• word pairs; -tion pattern

VISUAL COMMUNICATION
Create a Poster

Assessment

• create a variety of media works

LINK TO CURRICULUM

LANGUAGE ARTS
Write Away for Information

SOCIAL STUDIES
Check for Wheelchair Accessibility

Find Out About Special Games

PHYSICAL EDUCATION
Try Basketball Skills in a Sitting Position

Key Learning Expectations

Students will
• explain their interpretation of a written work, supporting it with evidence from the work and from their own knowledge and experience **(Reading Focus, p. 65)**
• read a variety of fiction and non-fiction materials for different purposes **(Reading Mini Lesson, p. 65)**
• produce pieces of writing using a variety of forms **(Writing Mini Lesson, p. 66)**
• create a variety of media works **(Visual Communication Mini Lesson, p. 67)**

LINK TO EXPERIENCE

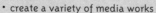

Talk About Being in a Wheelchair

Ask students to think about people they know or have heard about who are in a wheelchair, and invite them to share a bit about those people: how long they've been in a wheelchair, what kinds of things they can do, what they find difficult, what kind of a wheelchair they have, how they feel about being in a wheelchair, and so on.

Following the discussion, students can write a reflection in their journals about what they think it would be like to be in a wheelchair and the kinds of things they would do to have fun.

Experience Basketball

Invite students to tell what they know about the game of basketball and how it is played. Then take students into the gym to participate in ball handling games and drills. Older students or community players could be invited to come in and act as coaches and/or to demonstrate some of the basketball skills.

In discussion later, students can share which things they tried that would be the easiest to learn and which would require a lot of practice.

READ AND RESPOND TO TEXT

Reading Focus

Using a **read and paraphrase** strategy, have students read the article and, in writing, paraphrase the important or main information in each section. You may want to model this strategy with the group, using the first section. In pairs, they can share their writing and talk about whether they have included the main ideas and important details of each section. Encourage them to add any missing information or delete any unnecessary details.

Lighting Up

The Mini Lights are a wheelchair basketball team for kids 6 to 12. The team started in 1987. There are 18 players on the team. They practise on Saturday mornings. They play against each other and do demonstration games.

Reader Response

Students could
- make an outline of the article, following the format introduced in "Helping Hands," using the headings in the selection as the main outline headings. They could also refer to Learning Strategy Card 9, *Making an Outline*.
- take the role of one of the Mini Lights in a conversation he/she might have at school, telling about wheelchair basketball.
- write literal, inferential, and evaluative questions about the article to ask another student.
- find/read stories, biographies, autobiographies, and magazine or newspaper articles about people who are physically disabled, such as Terry Fox, Rick Hansen, Joni Eareckson Tada, Christopher Reeves.
- write a response to the article describing their feelings about the Mini Lights kids.

REVISIT THE TEXT

Reading

Read a Newspaper Article

Blackline Master 13

Read aloud the paragraph in "Hot Wheels" that introduces Alexander Curtis, the player who first joined the Mini Lights as their youngest player and has now moved up to the Junior Lights

▶

Get Ready to Read

Introduce this next selection by its title and ask students to suggest what connection this title might have with the game of basketball. As they read the story, they can check their predictions.

ONGOING
ASSESSMENT

Consider:
☐ Can the students pick out the most important information in each section?
☐ Can the students paraphrase the information using mostly their own words?

Blackline Master 13

Blackline Master 14

team. Then have students read carefully the newspaper article on Blackline Master 13, *Hot Wheels and Hoops*, and jot down new information they learn about Alex.

Together, discuss how the information in the article provides a greater understanding of Alex, his family, and his activities. Talk about which pieces of information are important details about Alex and which are just details that make the article more interesting to read.

Students can write a paragraph about Alexander, combining information from the anthology selection and the newspaper article. In small groups, they can read their paragraphs aloud, comparing the pieces of information they chose to include.

Writing

Write an Article with Headings

Blackline Master 14

Review with the students the use of headings in an article by having them look again at "Hot Wheels!," "Moments and Memories," and "Helping Hands." Talk about how the paragraphs grouped under each heading have a common focus, and how the heading reflects the main idea in a short, catchy phrase.

Make an overhead transparency of the article about Rick Hansen on Blackline Master 14, and work together as a group to write headings for this article. First, decide upon appropriate breaks in the article by grouping paragraphs together that have a common focus. Talk about the main idea of each grouping, and invite students to suggest related headings. Ask volunteers to read aloud each section of the article while others listen, and as a group select the best heading for each section.

In pairs, or on their own, students can write an article and use headings to focus the information for themselves as authors and for their readers. Possibilities for their writing might be:
- topics they can research such as spina bifida, the Terry Fox Run, Rick Hansen's Man in Motion Tour, the Special Olympics, types of wheelchairs, …,.
- an article about a person they know who is in a wheelchair.

Blackline Master 24   • word pairs; -tion pattern

Explore and Discover

Use Blackline Master 24 and the **sort**, **share**, **discuss**, and **chart** procedure outlined on page 16 to work with the words.

Talk about the different word pairs, noting how most of them are opposites. Have students use the dictionary to look up "practice" and "practise" to see when each can be used. Ongoing charts can be started for words of similar spellings and for opposites. Read aloud the words with "tion" while students clap out the syllables, and note that "tion" is a separate syllable. Together, list other words with the same sound that may have the "tion" or "ion" spelling.

Follow this exploration with a **pretest**, **study and practise**, and a **post test** as outlined on page 16.

Study and Practise

Students could
• use Learning Strategy Card 3 to study words identified after the pretest.
• prepare for a spelling quiz with a partner by looking at each word card, spelling the word quietly, and tracing over the spelling pattern with a colored marker. The partners then exchange cards and ask each other to spell the words.
• write five of the words three times, putting a blank in place of letters that present difficulty. Then they fill in the blanks and write the word without looking at the practice words.

Visual Communication

Create a Poster

Learning Strategy Card 10

Imagine that the Mini Lights are coming to your school for a demonstration game, and students are to design a poster advertising the event. To help them plan their poster-making, you can
• use Learning Strategy Card 10.
• brainstorm a list of tips for poster-making and jot these on chart paper for reference.

You might wish to show students samples of posters advertising events to help them with their ideas.

Arrange students in pairs to create a poster. Suggest that they revisit the selection to pull out any information they could use in the poster, and make up any information that they will still need.

 Assessment   See **Assess Learning**, page 69.

HOT WHEELS!

• word pairs; -tion pattern

demonstration	operation
condition	practice
junior	practise
special	regulation
regular	senior
younger	older

Theme/Challenge Words

• people words

athletes	society	physical
self-esteem	confidence	

Early Words

• high utility words (irregular spellings)

gone	lose	though
move	none	

MINI LIGHTS IN ACTION

How much: $2.00 ticket

where: University gym
when: wed. Jan8 1:00-5:00

LINK TO CURRICULUM

Language Arts

Write Away for Information

Students can write to the Alberta Northern Lights to get further information about their activities and basketball program, or to ask about contacting one of the players and becoming a pen pal. They would address their inquiries to:

> Alberta Northern Lights
> Wheelchair Basketball Society
> 6792 - 99 Street
> Edmonton, Alberta T6E 5B8

Or they might like to write for information to an organization within their community that works with disabled people.

The Internet provides information on team statistics and about the Northern Lights team players. Students could enter the key words **Alberta Northern Lights** in an Internet search engine.

Social Studies

Check for Wheelchair Accessibility

In a large group, students could organize a research project on wheelchair accessibility. They might begin by brainstorming a number of questions that come to mind and build some of their research around these. Activities such as these could be part of their research:

- Think about what they do in a single day and consider what adaptations would need to be made to allow them to get about in a wheelchair.
- Check into what makes a building wheelchair accessible.
- Look around their school, community centre, shopping area/centre, restaurants, and so on to see if someone in a wheelchair would be able to manage.
- Make a floor plan or map showing the route a person in a wheelchair might have to take to get to various places in their school or community.
- Find out where people in wheelchairs sit in places such as the local theatre and hockey arena, and how they get on the bus.

The group could then split into smaller groups, with each taking responsibility for one area of research. The groups could compile their information into one presentation with charts, written and oral information, photos, or another form of their choice. They may also wish to write letters to certain community places, commending some on their wheelchair accessibility and asking others to consider making accommodations.

A related homework project is to make a presentation about an athlete or team. See *Home Connections Newsletter*, Blackline Master 2.

Find Out About Special Games

Students could find out about one of the many special athletic events held for disabled people around the world and in Canada. Some possibilities are:
– the Paralympics (Olympics for the Physically Disabled)
– World Winter Games for the Physically Disabled
– World Aquatic Championships for the Physically Disabled
– Pan Am Games for the Disabled
Students could share their findings in an oral or written report, in an illustrated chart, or in a comparison chart for one of these games and another game not for the disabled, such as the Olympics or Commonwealth Games.

Physical Education

Try Basketball Skills in a Sitting Position

In the gym or outside, set up opportunities for students to try basketball skills from a chair. Students can try some of the following practice activities of the Mini Lights and can also think of some themselves:
• shooting into plastic garbage cans
• throwing the ball against a wall or backboard to try chest passes
• in two facing chairs several feet apart, trying bounce passes
• dribbling the ball, trying first with one hand and then the other

Following the chair activities, students can talk about the experience—whether they found it frustrating, how long they think they would need to practise to get good at the skills, and so on.

A s s e s s   L e a r n i n g

Visual Communication

(see p. 67)

Students can **peer assess** each other's posters in pairs. Develop with the students criteria for the assessment, using the guidelines they developed for posters. Students could write their assessments first, then discuss them. Assessors should sign the assessment sheets, and students can keep them for reference.

Assessing Posters

Student's name: _____ Date _____

	Yes	Needs Work
1. Does the poster give all the necessary information?	☐	☐
2. Does this information stand out? Is it easy to read?	☐	☐
3. Do the pictures give information? Do they fit with the poster?	☐	☐
4. Is the poster well designed? Is it attractive?	☐	☐

Comments

The Hockey Song

This selection features "The Hockey Song," written by Stompin' Tom Connors. Its descriptive and action-packed language and its catchy chorus make it fun to read, listen to, and sing.

Anthology, pages 50-51

Learning Choices

LINK TO EXPERIENCE

Listen to a Story

List Words Related to Hockey

READ AND RESPOND TO TEXT

READING FOCUS
• read a variety of fiction and non-fiction materials for different purposes
• STRATEGY: **listen and visualize**

Assessment

REVIST THE TEXT

mini LESSONS

READING
Consider a Songwriter's Techniques
• identify various forms of writing and identify their characteristics

Assessment

WRITING
Write a Song About a Team Sport
• produce media texts using writing and materials from other media

ORAL COMMUNICATION
Simulate a Sports Broadcast
• use tone of voice, gestures, and other non-verbal cues to help clarify meaning when making a presentation

LINK TO CURRICULUM

LANGUAGE ARTS
Compare a Book and a Video

THE ARTS
Draw a Team Crest

SOCIAL STUDIES
Learn About a Songwriter

Research Sports Equipment

MATHEMATICS
Take a Hockey Survey

Key Learning Expectations

Students will
• read a variety of fiction and non-fiction materials for different purposes **(Reading Focus, p. 71)**
• identify various forms of writing and identify their characteristics **(Reading Mini Lesson, p. 72)**
• produce media texts using writing and materials from other media **(Writing Mini Lesson, p. 72)**
• use tone of voice, gestures, and other non-verbal cues to help clarify meaning when making a presentation **(Oral Communication Mini Lesson, p. 73)**

LINK TO EXPERIENCE

Listen to a Story

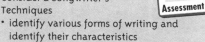

Read aloud a hockey story, such as the classic, *The Hockey Sweater*, and have students talk about the story itself and other hockey topics such as hockey "greats" and the NHL hockey league.

Invite the students to set up a classroom hockey library with books from home or from the public and/or school libraries. They could also bring in hockey cards, game programs, and other hockey memorabilia to display along with the books.

READ-ALOUD HOCKEY STORIES

Hockey Night In Transcona. John Danakas. Lorimer, 1995.

The Hockey Sweater. Roch Carrier. Tundra, 1984.

The Moccasin Goalie. William Roy Brownridge. Orca, 1995.

The Night They Stole the Stanley Cup. Roy MacGregor. McClelland & Stewart, 1995.

Two Minutes for Roughing. Joseph Romain. Lorimer, 1994.

List Words Related to Hockey

Have students brainstorm words or phrases related to the game of hockey. List these words on the board or an overhead transparency, then have them suggest categories their words would fit into. Decide upon headings for these categories and write each of the headings at the top of a piece of paper.

Put students into groups, giving each group one of the heading papers. In their groups, they can select appropriate words and phrases from the brainstorm list and write them on the sheet, along with others they can think of. The completed category lists can then be posted on the bulletin board. Encourage students to add to the lists over time.

 # READ AND RESPOND TO TEXT

Reading Focus

 Use a **listen and visualize** strategy. Play the *COLLECTIONS 5* audio version, or a CD or cassette version of "The Hockey Song," or read the selection to students. You may want to invite a guest reader or singer to the classroom for this activity.

Ask students to listen to the song and jot down words or phrases that create pictures in their minds. Read or play the song a second time so they can check their jot notes and add to them if they wish. Then have them form small groups to talk about the song, tell about the pictures they saw in their minds, and share the words that helped create those images.

Have students choose an image they have in their minds and sketch an illustration of it. They can then share their illustrations with a partner, and, looking at the selection, talk about where their pictures fit into the text and why.

 See **Assess Learning**, page 75.

Reader Response

Students could
- do a finished drawing of their sketch and incorporate into the picture words from the part of the song the drawing is about.
- write a short paragraph telling what effect songs like this, and cheering, and "the wave" have on the crowd and the team at a sporting event.
- talk with some classmates about the Stanley Cup and discuss what it might mean to a team to be winners of this award.
- get the picture book version of *Hockey Night Tonight: The Hockey Song* from the library and compare it with the version in the anthology.
 • talk with some family members about great hockey experiences, either as a fan or as a player.

Get Ready to Read

To introduce this selection, ask students if they have ever heard a recording of the "The Hockey Song" or have heard it sung at an NHL hockey game. Explain that this song is written by a songwriter from the Maritimes who has become well known for writing simple, down-to-earth songs about things people know well.

"The Hockey Song," performed by Stompin' Tom, is available from EMI Music Canada on the following albums:
- *Stompin' Tom and The Hockey Song*
- *Once Upon A Stompin' Tom*
- *Kic* Along With Stompin' Tom*
It is also performed by The Goods, on the album *Contact! The Canadian All Star Collection*.

* Keep It Canadian

Hockey Night Tonight: The Hockey Song and *Bud the Spud* are two Stompin' Tom books available from Ragweed Press.

REVISIT THE TEXT

Reading

Consider a Songwriter's Techniques

Have students read the song to find examples of techniques the writer used that helped make the song exciting and enjoyable to listen to. Guide them in finding and articulating examples such as the following:

Rhyme
- some lines rhyme at the end
- some internal rhyme within the lines of the stanzas

Rhythm
- definite beat

Structure
- 3 stanzas (one for each period of play)
- chorus repeated after each stanza

Repetition
- of the chorus
- of the phrase "the good old hockey game"

Language
- similes: "storm the crease like bumblebees," "travel like a burning flame"
- picturesque language: "skates aflash," "go bursting up," "final flick of a hockey stick," "one gigantic scream"

Talk about how the similes and picturesque language are effective in portraying the action, excitement, and tension of the game.

Arrange the students in pairs or small groups to write the words to a song they know or look at one in a music book. Have them note any similar techniques used by other songwriters and any new techniques they find.

You may also want to talk about the similarities between techniques used in writing poems and songs. Then students could choose a poem to note techniques.

Writing

Write a Song About a Team Sport

Building on what students discovered about the techniques used by the songwriter in "The Hockey Song," work with them to write a new ending to the third verse that makes the game end in a tie at the end of regulation time. They could then go on to write a new fourth verse about a win in overtime.

Invite students to think of another team sport they enjoy or to recall an exciting hockey game they've been to or played in. They can use some of the techniques used by Stompin' Tom Connors to write their own action song or poem.

ONGOING
ASSESSMENT

Consider:

☐ Can the students locate examples of the songwriter's techniques?

☐ Are they able to express how these techniques help in picturing and appreciating the action of the song?

There's one last shot,
the centre's hot,
But it whizzes past the net.
Fans groan and cry,
the score stays tied,
The good old hockey game.

Oral Communication

Simulate a Sports Broadcast

Tape-record a few minutes of a hockey broadcast from the radio or television to play for the students. Ask them to listen closely to note things about the broadcaster's way of speaking, such as voice inflections, variety of sentences, descriptions of plays, and so on. Discuss what they noticed about the broadcast and, together, make a list of things they think make an effective sports broadcast.

With the students, read the account of the opening period in the first stanza of the song and plan with jot notes what a sports broadcaster might say in a play-by-play description of some of the action. Invite a few students to take the role of a broadcaster and "broadcast" some of the plays. The other students can listen and comment on things that are effective and things that could be improved upon.

In small groups, students can plan play-by-play broadcasts of the other periods or choose another sport or game. The broadcasts could be recorded on tape, complete with background music and sound effects if wanted, and played for the whole group for their enjoyment and critique.

When you do a Sports Broadcast, try
– to sound really excited
– to change the level of your voice; get loud when it's exciting
– not to talk too fast
– to use short sentences most of the time; sometimes just a few words
– to use words that describe the action
– to say players' names
– to tell exactly what's happening
– to tell interesting extras when there's time

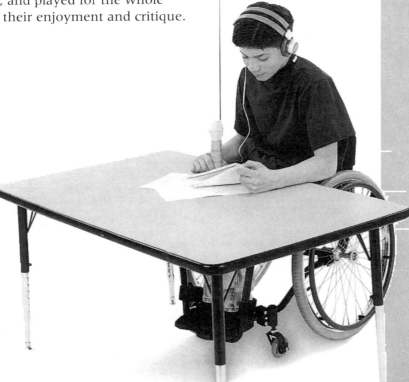

The Hockey Sweater, available from National Film Board Libraries, is a 10 minute animated version of the story. See pages 5 and (ii) for source information.

A print version of the story also appears in the Journeys 6 Anthology, *Ride the Wave*.

Consider inviting a local songwriter or two to class to sing and to talk about their craft.

Language Arts

Compare a Book and a Video

If the students did not listen to a reading of *The Hockey Sweater* previously, they can read it now. Then show the National Film Board video of the book. In small groups, students can talk about the similarities and differences between the two and the things they liked better in one than in the other.

The Arts

Draw a Team Crest

With the help of the students, set up a display of crests, using pictures and actual crests and sweaters. Invite students to talk about the crests—the team or group they are for and what the letters and/or symbols in the crest represent. Students can then create a crest for a team of their choice, whether real or imaginary, and write an accompanying explanation of the symbols.

Social Studies

Learn About a Songwriter

In pairs, students can refer to a variety of resources to learn about Stompin' Tom Connors and his music to write a report about him. They might use such sources as books, information on CD and tape cases, the Internet, and CBC radio. They could also select a few favorite songs of his to use in their presentations to the class.

Research Sports Equipment

Students could choose a sport and research the equipment needed. They could draw a picture of a player wearing the equipment, along with identifying labels. Information about the different pieces and reasons for each one could be written underneath the diagram. Post the completed diagrams in the classroom.

Mathematics

Take a Hockey Survey

In small groups, students could plan a set of questions to use in a school survey about hockey.

Once the survey questions are finalized, students should decide which students and how many students they will survey; for example 10 boys and 10 girls each from Grades 4, 5, and 6. After the survey, each group can represent their information on a graph of their choice to summarize the results. The graphs can be posted in the hallway for students who participated in the survey to read and analyze.

- Do you play hockey?

- Do you go to watch hockey games where family or friends are playing?

- Do you watch hockey on TV?

- Have you been to an NHL game?

- Do you like hockey?

- Do you collect hockey cards?

A s s e s s   L e a r n i n g

Assessment

Reading Focus (see p. 71)

Select a small number of students' illustrations to use as **work samples** for assessment. Talk with each of the students about his/her illustration, asking questions such as:
– What part of the song is your picture about?
– How does your picture represent that part?
– What details did you include to show what that part meant to you?
– What did you like about those words of the song?
– How did they help you create the picture?
– Is there anything you would add to your picture?

The Big Game

This script, taken from The Herbie Jones Reader's Theater, tells the story of how the Laurel Beef baseball team scored an unexpected win when two players put in surprise performances.

Anthology, pages 52-59   Blackline Masters 15 and 16
Learning Strategy Card 11

Learning Choices

LINK TO EXPERIENCE

Tell About Baseball Experiences

Talk About Baseball Cards

READ AND RESPOND TO TEXT

READING FOCUS
• read a variety of fiction and non-fiction materials for different purposes
• STRATEGY: **double look**

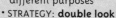 Assessment

REVISIT THE TEXT

READING
Learn About Readers' Theatre
• identify various forms of writing and describe their characteristics

WRITING
Write a Baseball Lingo File
• communicate ideas and information for a variety of purposes

ORAL COMMUNICATION
Perform a Readers' Theatre Script
• use appropriate structures in classroom presentations

Assessment

LINK TO CURRICULUM

LANGUAGE ARTS
Read a Poem

Create a Trivia Game

THE ARTS
Create a Cartoon

SCIENCE
Research Pitches

MATHEMATICS
Develop Baseball Statistics Problems

Key Learning Expectations

Students will
• read a variety of fiction and non-fiction materials for different purposes **(Reading Focus, p. 77)**
• identify various forms of writing and describe their characteristics **(Reading Mini Lesson, p. 78)**
• communicate ideas and information for a variety of purposes **(Writing Mini Lesson, p. 79)**
• use appropriate structures in classroom presentations **(Oral Communication Mini Lesson, p. 80)**

LINK TO EXPERIENCE

Tell About Baseball Experiences

Ask students to share their experiences with playing baseball,
• telling about the skills they found difficult/easy
• telling funny, embarrassing, or exciting stories
• describing variations of the game they've played
• recounting other anecdotes
Students could then draw a picture showing a memorable time when they played baseball, write in their journals about a memory associated with baseball, or continue talking with a partner about their baseball experiences.

Talk About Baseball Cards

Ask students to bring baseball cards they are willing to share with the class. With the help of students who know something about the statistic charts on the cards, talk about what the headings and the information mean. Have the students form small groups, each with a knowledgeable student, to look at a few cards and talk about the things they learned about the players from the cards. Students might be interested in finding out about the history of baseball cards. Or they could gather books that provide more information about the game and the players.

Baseball Card History
Back in 1887, tobacco companies included small baseball cards in packages of cigarettes. In the 1930s, most baseball cards were packaged with bubble gum.

Up until 1981, two manufacturing companies controlled all printing of cards. Now many companies can print baseball cards.

READ AND RESPOND TO TEXT

Reading Focus

Use a **double look** strategy. Have students read the script through for the first time to gain an understanding of the plot. Encourage them to talk in small groups about the events of the story and the final outcome: why the team probably wouldn't win the game, what events happened that made the difference, and what was the turning point in the story.

On the second reading, students can read in pairs to relate the plot action and the rise in excitement during the game to how the characters would speak. They could select several lines to read to one another, trying different voice inflections, volume, and pace of speaking to reflect the action of the plot.

Reader Response

Students could
- hold a conversation about the selection, discussing questions such as:
  - **Why do you think Herbie was given the name of Captain Whiff?**
  - **What did Annabelle mean when she said, "I'm a vacuum cleaner at first base"?**
  - **What effect do you think it had on Herbie when he heard his family yelling from the bleachers?**

  - **Who do you think the team should have cheered and carried on their shoulders at the end of the game? Why?**
- list all the things Annabelle did in her good luck ritual and talk with a partner about other good luck rituals they know about.
- write a description of one of the players on the Laurel Beef team.
- write a news report of the game.
- read additional stories about baseball or find out interesting information about baseball by reading related books.

BOOKS ABOUT BASEBALL

Curve Ball. John Danakas. Lorimer, 1993.

Baseball Legends. Bob Italia. Abdo, 1990.

A Day in the Life of a Baseball Player. Eric Arnold. Scholastic, 1996.

The Longest Home Run. Roch Carrier. Tundra, 1993.

Seventh Inning Stretch: Time-Out for Baseball Trivia. Brad Herzog. Bantam, 1994.

Touching All The Bases: Baseball for Kids of All Ages. Claire Mackay. Scholastic, 1994.

The Wagner Whacker. Joseph Romain. VanWell, 1996.

Get Ready to Read

Tell students they will be reading a readers' theatre script. Have them look at the first page of this selection to note the characters, setting, and time of the script. Then ask them to read the introduction and predict what might happen in the baseball game.

The Reading Mini Lesson identifies the structure and characteristics of readers' theatre, and the Listening/Speaking Mini Lesson helps students plan a performance.

ONGOING ASSESSMENT

Consider:

☐ Can students see the connection between characters, their actions, and events of the story?

☐ Are students able to relate to the story and read parts as the characters would speak?

REVISIT THE TEXT

Reading

Learn About Readers' Theatre

Learning Strategy Card 11

With the students, skim through the script, making notes on the board or overhead about text features of the script:

- characters, setting, and time listed at the beginning
- sound effects person included as a character with a part (SFX person)
- name of speaker written in capital, boldface letters before the words to be spoken
- words to be said with great emphasis are in capital letters
- sound effects are written in capital letters
- instructions to the characters about how to speak are written in italics and parentheses
- instructions for gestures of characters are written in italics and parentheses
- spaces between characters lines for ease of reading
- narrator provides extra information

Talk about how having the script set up in this way is helpful to those taking part in performing the readers' theatre and to the audience as well.

Provide other readers' theatre scripts that students can look through in small groups to see variations of script structure and features. They can share variations with the whole group and discuss preferences they might have and why. They could also read Learning Strategy Card 11, *Readers' Theatre*, for more ideas about readers' theatre and scripts.

Applying what they've just learned, students in small groups can write a readers' theatre script for another episode of the Laurel Beef team, or for one of the earlier anthology stories, or for another story they know. They can use their scripts to perform a readers' theatre for an audience following the suggestions set out in the Listening/Speaking Mini Lesson.

READERS' THEATRE SCRIPTS

The Herbie Jones Reader's Theatre. Suzy Kline. Putnam, 1992.

Presenting Reader's Theatre: Plays and Poems to Read Aloud. Caroline Feller Bauer. H. W. Wilson, 1987.

Writing

Write a Baseball Lingo File

Have students go through the selection, picking out as many baseball terms and expressions as they can find and jot them on the board. Ask them to add any others they know to the list. Then write each word or phrase on a file card.

Select a few of the words/phrases to work with in modelling the content for the file cards. Ask students to read aloud the part of the story where the word/phrase is used and explain the meaning using context clues and their prior knowledge. They could also use references for those not in the script and to verify their ideas. Together, write a definition on the card. Students might also like to include an illustration that exemplifies the definition.

Give individuals or pairs of students a baseball lingo file card and have them complete the card following the modelled approach. As the cards are finished, place them in a file box in alphabetical order. Some students could make an index card, alphabetically listing all the terms and expressions, to place at the front of the file set.

To assist students in determining the meaning of baseball lingo and learning about aspects of the game, you could
— have reference books on hand
— invite a resource person into the class for a question and answer period
— ask students to talk to a knowledgeable family member or friend

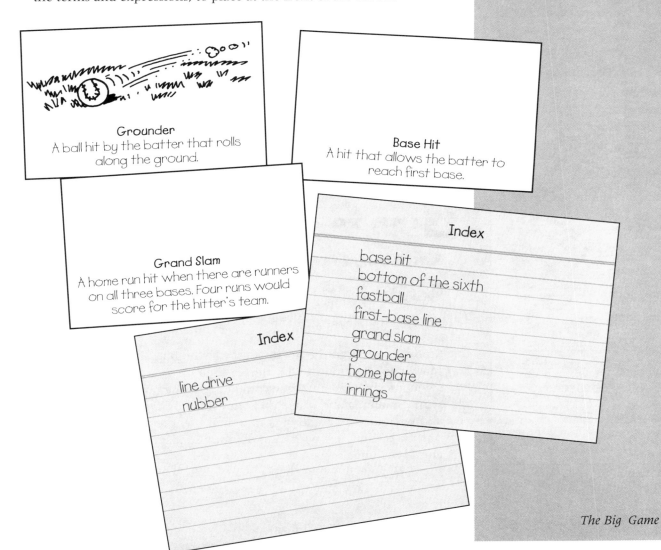

Grounder
A ball hit by the batter that rolls along the ground.

Base Hit
A hit that allows the batter to reach first base.

Grand Slam
A home run hit when there are runners on all three bases. Four runs would score for the hitter's team.

Index

line drive
nubber

Index

base hit
bottom of the sixth
fastball
first-base line
grand slam
grounder
home plate
innings

Oral Communication

Perform a Readers' Theatre Script

Describe readers' theatre as a dramatic reading that can be very simple. With the students, talk about how a reading of "The Big Game" might be effectively and simply performed, using the script features, information on Learning Strategy Card 11, and their own prior knowledge. Bring out points such as

- readers usually sit or stand together, facing the audience
- they read from a script, but look up often to make eye contact with audience
- they do not move or gesture, unless the gesture is a simple hand movement that goes along with the words
- they use their voices to express emotions and carry the action of the plot
- they may wear regular clothes or dress alike in something simple like dark shirts and jeans
- they may use a few simple "character props," such as sunglasses or scarves
- no stage props or scenery are used, but a plain curtain or backdrop can be used to set the scene or create a mood

Discuss how more elaborate productions may be done using sound effects (as in this script), music, more props, and so on, but emphasize that it is the readers' voices that are most important in doing readers' theatre.

Keeping these points in mind, students can work in groups to practise and perform "The Big Game" or one of the scripts they wrote in small groups.

Assessment   See **Assess Learning**, page 82.

LINK TO CURRICULUM

Language Arts

Read a Poem

Blackline Master 15

Students can read the poem "Casey at the Bat," on Blackline Master 15, to find out why Herbie used Casey as an example of someone striking out. They could discuss the poem with a partner, talking about whether they liked or didn't like the poem and why, or they could illustrate their favorite part of the poem, or they could work with a small group to plan and present a choral reading.

Blackline Master 15

Create a Trivia Game

Students might like to create a trivia game about baseball or another game of their choice. Suggest that they first brainstorm a number of questions about the game, then divide up the questions among individuals or pairs who will conduct research to find the answers, using books such as those listed in the Bookbag on page 77. As they look for the answers, they might find interesting tidbits that they want to include in the game. Suggest that they write questions for these answers and include them in the game.

Students can write the questions on one side of a card, and the answers on the other. They can play a trivia game with the cards, devising a set of rules for the game. They can also share their game with other classes.

Questions for a trivia game must be very specific and have only one possible answer. Also, there should be a good chance that the players will be able to answer some of the questions.

What player holds the record for the most home runs?

What Canadian team won the World Series?

What was the "Field of Dreams"?

What two leagues play in the World Series?

The Arts

Create a Cartoon

Invite students to draw a cartoon picture or strip about some amusing part of "The Big Game" or a baseball game they have watched or played. Remind them to use speech balloons and/or thought bubbles and captions to clearly recount the incident. These cartoons can be put up on the bulletin board for others to enjoy.

Science

Research Pitches

Blackline Master 16

Interested students can use a variety of resources—Blackline Master 16, *The Pitcher's Arsenal,* and people who know—to learn about different kinds of pitches and why they work the way they do. Suggest they practise the different pitches to get a better idea of how they work. Then, to share what they learn, they can demonstrate the pitches while explaining them.

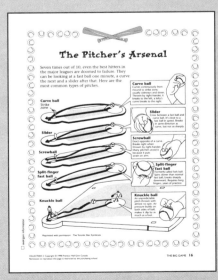

Blackline Master 16

> Babe Ruth held the record for home runs with 714 homers. Hank Aaron broke that record, then went on to hit 755 homers by the time he retired in 1976.
> 1. By how many did he beat Babe Ruth's record?
> 2. How many homers did they have altogether?
> 3. How many homers did they average between them?

Mathematics

Develop Baseball Statistics Problems

Students can gather statistics from baseball cards, game programs, books, newspapers, and sports magazines, and develop a set of problems using the information.

> The game of baseball was invented in the year 1839. How long has baseball been around?

Suggest that they write the problems on one side of a piece of paper, and show the steps used to arrive at the solution, along with a sentence with the answer on the other side. The question/answer sheets can be exchanged with other students, who try to solve the problem and then check their work.

Assessment

A s s e s s   L e a r n i n g

Oral Communication (see p. 80)

Watch students perform their readers' theatre script, and in each group, focus on a few students to assess using anecdotal notes. Comment on their use of voice and on their ability to interpret and follow the script.

Date: October 5

Student: Samira

Readers' Theatre Script: group's created script about family baseball

Notes:
- came in on cue
- read clearly and loudly enough most of the time
- read a little too quickly when had a longer part
- sounded really excited when she was cheering her brother on
- got a little too excited once and started to read the next speaker's part
- made eye contact once, but lost her place

Teaching Plan: work on reading ahead in your mind; will help with making eye contact and noting where to stop reading

---

THEME: WORKING TOGETHER AS A TEAM

Anthology, pages 60-61

Team Spirit — *an acrostic poem and commentary*

Hockey — *a poem*

Teamwork — *an essay*

My Baseball Game — *a personal narrative*

Good Try — *a story*

LINK TO THE THEME

After reading, the students could
• use cutouts from magazines and newspapers to make a collage poster about one of the team activities mentioned in the writing or another sport of their choice.
• in a small group, role-play a team pre-game gathering in which they talk about the game and encourage each other.

LINK TO THE WRITING PROCESS

Write About Sporting Behavior

Students could work in pairs to reread "Teamwork" and note suggestions in the piece for being a fair sports player. Have them add any ideas of their own, as well as ideas about behaviors of a fair sports fan. They can use their notes to write a paragraph(s) to persuade people to behave and think in a sporting manner. Encourage them to give reasons for their opinions. The paragraphs could be shared with other pairs to gather ideas for revisions, and the final writings posted in a school hallway.

Language Workshop — Grammar

• use correctly the conventions of grammar (verbs)

Blackline Master 17

Teach/Explore/Discover

Read aloud the poem "Hockey," while students follow along. Ask them to note the action words (verbs) in the first four lines. Then ask them to move these verbs in front of the things

(nouns) they now follow—flying sticks, roaring crowds, scored goals, frustrated goalies—to see that these verbs are really describing the noun. Explain that verbs that end in "ing" or "ed" are special verbs because they can be both a verb and a describing word (adjective).

Write a list of words on the board, for example, "puppies," "classmates," "movies," "houses," and ask the students to brainstorm verbs that could be used to describe these things. Tell them that the special verb is usually in front of the noun when used in a complete sentence.

Practise/Apply

Students could
• complete Blackline Master 17, *Special Verbs*.
• use the noun/special verb pattern of "Hockey" to write a poem about another sport.

Blackline Master 17

Our Swim Team

Swimmers crouching
Water splashing
Arms stroking
Feet kicking
Bodies surging
We race down the lanes.

LINK TO THE WRITER

Reread Natalie's comments with the students to note that she explained why she liked writing. Ask students to complete the following phrase in their journals and share their thoughts with a partner if they wish.

I think writing is _____

_____

because _____.

The Last Dragon

In this picture book story by Susan Miho Nunes, Peter Chang spends his summer with his Great Aunt who lives in Chinatown. He buys a dragon hanging in a store window and works hard to bring the faded and ripped Last Dragon back to life.

Anthology, pages 62–70   Blackline Masters 18, 19, and 25

Learning Choices

LINK TO EXPERIENCE

Write About a Personal Memory

Talk About Completing Tasks

READ AND RESPOND TO TEXT

READING FOCUS
• describe how various elements **Assessment** in a story function
• STRATEGY: **guided listening or reading**

REVISIT THE TEXT

mini LESSONS

READING
Create a Story Map
• read a variety of fiction and non-fiction materials for different purposes

WRITING
Write a Work Plan   **Assessment**
• produce various pieces of writing using a variety of forms
Language Workshop — Spelling
• com; ex-, -ly patterns

VISUAL COMMUNICATION
Paint a Picture
• create a variety of media works

LINK TO CURRICULUM

LANGUAGE ARTS
Share Stories About Wise People

Learn About the Dragon Dance

SOCIAL STUDIES
Make a Community Services Directory

SCIENCE
Research Herbs

Key Learning Expectations

Students will
• describe how various elements in a story function **(Reading Focus, p. 85)**
• read a variety of fiction and non-fiction materials for different purposes **(Reading Mini Lesson, p. 85)**
• produce various pieces of writing using a variety of forms **(Writing Mini Lesson, p. 86)**
• create a variety of media works **(Visual Communication Mini Lesson, p. 87)**

LINK TO EXPERIENCE

Write About a Personal Memory

As a group, the students can discuss times when they were bored and what made them feel bored. They might suggest such things as:
– when friends were away and there was no one to play with
– visiting relatives and there was nothing to do
– a rainy day when they had to stay indoors

Invite the students to write about a time they were bored and what they did, if anything, to solve the problem. Encourage them to reflect on what they might have done to ease the boredom. They could share their writing with a partner if they wish.

Talk About Completing Tasks

Have students imagine they have been given an important task to make forest scenery for a play. The scenery would need to cover a space about the size of a large bulletin board. Ask them what they could do/plan to make sure that they do all the things that need to be done to complete the task. They might suggest:
– keep a detailed list of what has to be done
– remember things in their heads
– list things in order of the way they are to be done
– plan a schedule so that each part of the task gets done on time
– get others to help
– draw a sketch of what the scenery will look like when its finished

Students could work in pairs to complete a detailed plan for the task and then share their ideas with other students.

READ AND RESPOND TO TEXT

Reading Focus

Blackline Master 18

 Use the **guided listening or reading** strategy. Read the story aloud or have students read on their own. Some students may choose to listen to the *COLLECTIONS 5* audio version. At designated pause points, ask the students to identify the problem Peter encountered in repairing the dragon and what kind of solution he came up with in order to solve the challenge.

Provide students with Blackline Master 18, *Problems and Solutions Chart*, to jot their ideas. (The first pause point has been completed as a model.) After the reading, they can share their problem/solution charts within a small group to compare what they have written. Suggest that they refer to the selection to prove/change their ideas.

Problems and Solutions Chart

Pause Point	Problem	Solution
Great Aunt shrugged. "Humph. Couldn't have his mouth hanging open like a fool."	- the dragon's mouth was broken - it had no teeth	- the aunt fixed the mouth so it wouldn't hang open - she combed its whiskers - she polished the pearl
When Peter asked about the dragon's body, Mr. Pang said, "Don't be impatient. This is a big job."		
"No problem," said Miss Rose Chiao, "but I could use a hand once or twice a week."		
"They must be blessed by a priest, or the dragon will never see."		
"Why, he looks fierce enough to cause a typhoon."		
"Can he see with these?" he asked. "Very soon," said Great Aunt, "very soon."		
The Last Dragon's eyes raked the room from side to side. A drum began to beat.		

COLLECTIONS 5 Copyright © 1998 Prentice Hall Ginn Canada.
Permission to reproduce this page is restricted to the purchasing school.

THE LAST DRAGON 18

Blackline Master 18

Reader Response

Students could
- read the story again, independently.
- read other books about children discovering their cultural roots.
- draw a favorite character from the story and write why this was a favorite character.
- write about a lesson they learned from reading the story.
- make a list of things in the story that they found unique or different.

REVISIT THE TEXT

Reading

Create A Story Map

Blackline Master 19

Using Blackline Master 19, *Story Map*, work together with the students to summarize the plot of the story. Prepare an overhead transparency and/or copies for the students. Have students complete the parts of the map independently and then share their ideas. Complete the map on the overhead according to class consensus.

▶

Get Ready to Read

Write the title on the board and ask students to predict what the story might be about. List their ideas on the board so they can see after reading how accurate their predictions were.

ONGOING ASSESSMENT

Consider:

☐ Is the information on the students' charts relevant to the story?

☐ Do students refer to their charts during group discussions?

☐ Can the students find proof in the story for their ideas?

BOOKS ABOUT CHILDREN DISCOVERING THEIR CULTURAL ROOTS

Chin Chiang and the Dragon's Dance. Ian Wallace. Douglas & McIntyre, 1984.

Have a Happy...: A Novel. Mildred Pitts Walter. Lothrop, Lee and Shepard, 1989.

Latkes and Applesauce: A Hanukkah Story. Fran Manushkin. Scholastic, 1990.

Mary McLean and the St. Patrick's Day Parade. Steven Kroll. Scholastic, 1991.

Rechenka's Eggs. Patricia Polacco. Philomel, 1988.

While Shepherds Watched. Jenni Fleetwood. Lothrop, Lee & Shepard, 1992.

Blackline Master 19

A related homework project is to carry out a special project with family and/or friends. See *Home Connections Newsletter*, Blackline Master 2.

Discuss how this map could be used with other stories they have read, such as "A Morning to Polish and Keep," "How I Got My Dogsled," and "Shelter Folks," and invite partners to choose a story and complete a story map for it.

Have the partners share and compare their completed story maps with another pair of students who chose the same story.

Writing

Write a Work Plan

Tell the students that they are going to write a work plan that would help Peter keep track of all the things that he must do to complete the repairs of the dragon. Explain that working plans can be written in a variety of ways. For example, Peter's tasks could be

- **organized by sequence**—the tasks must follow a specific order of completion.
- **organized by time**—the task requiring the most time would be listed first, and the rest in descending order of time needed.
- **organized by "who"**—tasks could be listed according to who is doing or helping with the task.
- **organized by importance**—tasks could be listed from most important to least important.

Have the students work with a partner or small group to first list all the tasks Peter needed to complete, and then develop a work plan. They may wish to organize their work plan using one of ways discussed, or choose one of their own.

Post the work plans for everyone to see. As a group, discuss the work plans using questions such as
- Which plan would be the easiest for Peter to follow? Why?
- Is there one style of organizing a work plan that appears more popular than the others? Why do you think that is?
- What would be your favorite style of planning? Why?

Students can then individually develop a work plan based on something that they themselves might need to plan; for example, a patrol party, a tea for parents, arranging for a speaker to visit the class, a bake sale.

 See **Assess Learning**, page 89.

Language Workshop — Spelling

Blackline Master 25 • com-, ex-, -ly patterns

Explore and Discover

Use Blackline Master 25 and the **sort**, **share**, **discuss**, and **chart** procedure outlined on page 16 to work with the words.

With the students, make word webs showing words with the syllables "com," "ex," and "ly." Then look at words such as "explained," "exclaimed," and "complained" that have similar letter combinations. Write these words, one under the other, highlighting and underlining the differences and similarities.

exclaimed
explained
complained

Follow this exploration with a **pretest**, **study and practise**, and a **post test** as outlined on page 16.

Study and Practise

Students could

- use Learning Strategy Card 3 to study words identified after the pretest.
- on their word cards, highlight any root words and print them on the back of the card.
- print their words on graph paper in order of shortest to longest. They

e	x	a	c	t	l	y	
c	o	m	p	a	n	y	
e	x	a	m	i	n	e	d
c	e	r	t	a	i	n	l	y

print one word per row, putting a letter in each square. To make it easier to read, they can leave a blank row between words.

Visual Communication

Paint a Picture

mini LESSON

With the students, revisit the illustrations in the story and/or in other selections and discuss the illustrator's attention to:

Originality

- Does the illustration fit with the selection?
- Does it capture the mood/feeling of the selection?
- Is the style (realistic, imaginary) appropriate for the selection?

Use of Detail

- Does the detail add to or supplement the information/ideas in the selection?
- Do the details come from the selection, from the illustrator's imagination, or from both?

▶

THE LAST DRAGON

• com-, ex-, -ly patterns

companions	thoughtfully
commotion	explained
crookedly	excitement
certainly	company
complained	exactly
examined	exclaimed

Theme/Challenge Words

• creature/person words

alien	creature	skeleton
companion	associate	

Early Words

• two-syllable words

dragon	about	artist
painter	began	

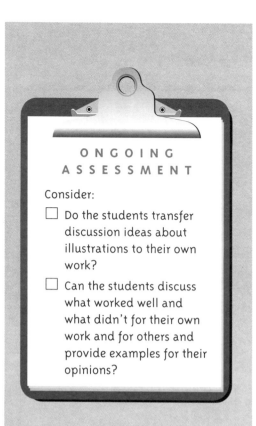

ONGOING
ASSESSMENT

Consider:

☐ Do the students transfer discussion ideas about illustrations to their own work?

☐ Can the students discuss what worked well and what didn't for their own work and for others and provide examples for their opinions?

Use of Page/Space

   – Does the illustration use the space provided?

   – Are the different elements of the illustration proportionate to each other? Are some too big or too small?

Have the students paint a picture of the dragon for this story or an illustration for another story using any painting technique that they think fits with their illustration, such as brush painting, fingerpainting, and so on.

Students could come together as groups of four where they would share their paintings and ask for input about how well they did in using the criteria to guide their work. Then display the paintings.

LINK TO CURRICULUM

Language Arts

Share Stories About Wise People

The students could write about the wisest person they know, providing examples that show the person's wisdom. Their stories could be displayed at the Writing Centre. Or, they may prefer to make a taped recording of their story and place the tape in the Listening Centre for their classmates to enjoy.

Learn About the Dragon Dance

Invite a speaker in to talk about the dragon dance or, if possible, dancers who could perform the dragon dance. Or, you could invite speakers and/or performers who could talk about/demonstrate some other aspect of Chinese culture.

To document the speaker's visit and/or the performers' dance, students could write up a short review and indicate what they enjoyed best about the experience.

Social Studies

Make a Community Services Directory

Invite the students to work together to make a directory of the services available in their community. These services could include business as well as government and community agencies. Suggest they start by brainstorming all the services they are familiar with. Then, they might take a walk around the community with family members to gather more information.

The directory should include the name of the service, a short description of the service it provides, the address, and phone number (which they can get from the phone book).

Science

Research Herbs

Students could research information about herbs. Suggest that they talk to family members about the herbs they use before looking to other sources. To assist them in organizing the information, they could design a chart where they could indicate which herbs are appropriate for cooking and which ones for medicinal purposes, with a short description of each. A T-chart might prove helpful in presenting their information.

Or, some students may prefer to research a particular herb and report on it. The information they include in their reports could cover such things as
– where the herb is found
– unique features of the herb
– how the herb came to be known
– why this particular herb appealed to them

HERBS

Food	Medicine
Catnip - Cats like the smell. When they eat it, they sometimes act a little crazy, or they go to sleep. Garlic - Garlic has a strong taste and smell. It's used as a flavoring in all kinds of dishes.	Garlic - It's used to help digestion of food. Ginseng - It gives people more energy and makes them feel better.

A s s e s s   L e a r n i n g

Assessment

Writing (see p. 86)

Choose five students to work with in **individual conferences** to assess how well they are able to construct a working plan. For each of the five students:
• ask them to explain the way in which they organized their plan and why they chose that way.
• ask them to explain how having this plan will enable them to complete the task more successfully.
• ask them to give examples of how their plan could be used for other tasks.
• record an anecdotal comment or grade indicating each student's proficiency in completing the task.

Last Chance for Cherry Tree Creek

In this story by Martin Silverstone from the magazine *Wild*, the children of the Lucas family discover that all the frogs in Cherry Tree Creek have died mysteriously. Together, with their mother and father, they set out to find out what happened to cause the death of the frogs.

Anthology, pages 71-77 Blackline Masters 20 and 25 Learning Strategy Car

Learning Choices

LINK TO EXPERIENCE

Identify Environmental Issues

Listen to a Story

READ AND RESPOND TO TEXT

READING FOCUS

• read a variety of fiction and non-fiction materials for different purposes
• STRATEGY: **narrated reading**

REVISIT THE TEXT

READING
Diagram Causes and Effects
• explain their interpretation of a written work, supporting it with evidence from the world and from their own knowledge and experience

WRITING
Write a Persuasive Letter
• communicate ideas and information for a variety of purposes
Language Workshop — Spelling
• adding endings; y to i; im pattern

ORAL COMMUNICATION
Discuss an Issue

• express and respond to ideas and opinions concisely, clearly, and appropriately

LINK TO CURRICULUM

LANGUAGE ARTS
Plan a Meeting

Find and Read a Variety of Materials

SCIENCE
Research an Ecosystem

ART
Design a Bulletin Board

Key Learning Expectations

Students will
• read a variety of fiction and non-fiction materials for different purposes (**Reading Focus, p. 91**)
• explain their interpretation of a written work, supporting it with evidence from the world and from their own knowledge and experience (**Reading Mini Lesson, p. 92**)
• communicate ideas and information for a variety of purposes (**Writing Mini Lesson, p. 93**)
• express and respond to ideas and opinions concisely, clearly, and appropriately (**Oral Communication Mini Lesson, p. 95**)

LINK TO EXPERIENCE

Identify Environmental Issues

Ask the students to reflect silently for a moment and think about the world they live in. Ask them to envision green grass, blue skies, clear waters, meadows, thick forests, …,.

With those images in their minds, have them think about some of the problems that are presently causing harm to the world's environment and creating a much different picture from the one in their minds. Record their ideas of the problems, then discuss them, using questions such as:
• Which of the problems listed would you consider to be the most harmful to the environment? Why?
• Which of these problems is happening in our community?
• What could be done to help solve the problems in our community?

Listen to a Story

Read aloud a story about an environmental issue from a child's perspective. Following the reading, ask the students to talk in small groups, and/or write in their journals about
• how this story made them feel and why.
• what they learned from the story.
• what they enjoyed best about the story.

Possible titles:

The Great Kapok Tree: A Tale of the Amazon Rain Forest by Lynne Cherry.

Jen and the Great One by Peter Evindyson.

Oliver Dibbs to the Rescue! by Barbara Steiner.

One World by Michael Foreman.

READ AND RESPOND TO TEXT

Reading Focus

Use the **narrated reading** strategy. Read aloud sections up to and including the sentence indicated in the suggested divisions. Stop and have the students discuss what might happen next and why they think so. Then have the students read on to the designated pause point, discuss what happened, and verify their predictions.

Suggested story divisions:

<u>Teacher read aloud</u>: *"He dropped the jug onto a pile of other containers on the ground and drove off."* [page 72] Stop, discuss, and predict.

<u>Student passage</u>: *"They disappear from clean water, too."* [page 74] Discuss and check predictions.

<u>Teacher read aloud</u>: *"First we have to let people know how serious the problem is, and then everyone has to work together to fix it."* [page74] Stop, discuss, and predict.

<u>Student passage</u>: *"Helen watched as they hurried off, smiled, and went back to her gardening."* [page 75] Discuss and check predictions.

<u>Teacher read aloud</u>: *"'Excuse me,'" she said softly, but everyone just kept arguing."* [page 76] Stop, discuss, and predict.

<u>Student passage</u>: *"'But don't forget, it's our home, too'"* [page 77] Discuss and check predictions.

After reading, ask the students to compare what they said they might do in the situation and what the Lucas family did. Invite the students to talk in small groups or pairs about the things that surprised them or parts of the story they particularly liked, and to read these parts aloud to each other.

Get Ready to Read

Ask the students what their reaction would be if they passed by a creek and discovered dozens of dead frogs. Ask them what they might do about it. Tell them that in this story, a family makes this very discovery and then decides to find the cause of the problem.

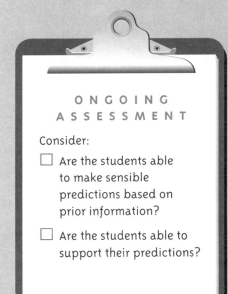

ONGOING ASSESSMENT

Consider:

☐ Are the students able to make sensible predictions based on prior information?

☐ Are the students able to support their predictions?

Reader Response

Students could
- hold a conversation about the story to discuss questions such as:
  - **What do you think the author was trying to tell readers by writing this story?**
  - **Do you approve of the way the family solved the problem? Why or why not?**
  - **What do you think would have happened if the Lucas family had not taken an interest in the problem at the creek?**
  - **Is there a character in the story you feel you are like? Who? How?**
- write a monologue about what they would like to say to one of the characters or to the group of adults who gathered at the meeting.
- draw a favorite scene from the story and write a caption for it.
- find and list words or phrases in the story that describe a healthy environment.

REVISIT THE TEXT

Reading

Diagram Causes and Effects

Explain to the students that writers use cause and effect patterns to tell readers why events happened or why things are as they are. Provide them with an example and discuss the pattern.

> "If you run in a busy hallway at school, what happens? You might bump into someone. Running is the cause and bumping into someone is the effect. Bumping into someone then might become the cause of another effect, such as the student you bumped into hurts his arm. Hurting an arm becomes a cause of something else, and so on."

Together with the students, diagram your example using a cause/effect organizer.

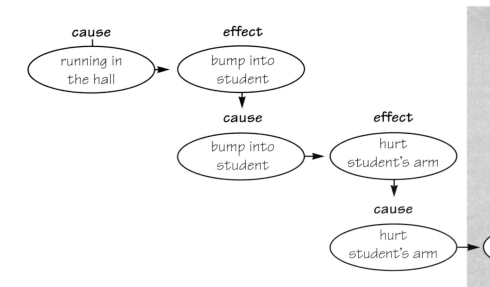

cause → effect
running in the hall → bump into student

cause → effect
bump into student → hurt student's arm

cause → effect
hurt student's arm → student goes to hospital

effect
student goes to hospital →

Have the students revisit the text, and with a partner, complete a cause and effect diagram for an incident from the story, for example:
– fertilizer put in the creek
– trees cut down on the shore
– the meeting is organized

Display the students' diagrams and encourage students to discuss and compare them.

Writing

Write a Persuasive Letter

Blackline Master 20
Learning Strategy Card 12

Explain that a persuasive letter is a way to influence people by stating your opinion about a problem and giving reasons why they should help to solve the problem, or at least convince them that the problem is important and they should be concerned about it.

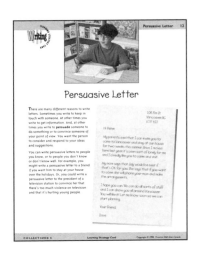

To help students understand the format of a persuasive letter, refer to Learning Strategy Card 12, *Persuasive Letter*. Or ask them to imagine that the letter is like a sandwich where the top layer states the problem/issue and your purpose, opinion, or request; the middle of the sandwich is where you give reasons for your opinion or request and support them with details; and the bottom layer of the sandwich restates your purpose and asks for support.

A PERSUASIVE LETTER SHOULD:

- state the problem/issue that the letter is about
- state the writer's purpose, opinion, or request about the problem/issue
- provide reasons or details that support the opinion/request
- restate the purpose and ask for support; provide details about the help the writer wants

▶

Blackline Master 20

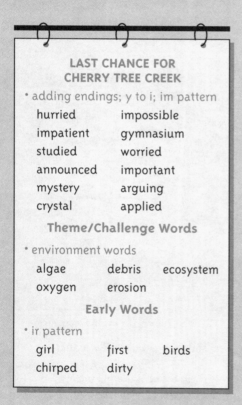

**LAST CHANCE FOR
CHERRY TREE CREEK**

• adding endings; y to i; im pattern

hurried	impossible
impatient	gymnasium
studied	worried
announced	important
mystery	arguing
crystal	applied

Theme/Challenge Words

• environment words

algae	debris	ecosystem
oxygen	erosion	

Early Words

• ir pattern

girl	first	birds
chirped	dirty	

Ask the students to think about the story and the issue of fertilizer being dumped into the creek. Provide them with copies of Blackline Master 20, *A Persuasive Letter*, or prepare an overhead transparency. Read the letter aloud, and ask students to listen/read for the three layers that make up a good persuasive letter.

After reading the letter, sketch an outline of the 3-layer organizer on the board. Ask students to fill in the layers with the appropriate information from the letter, and record their ideas in the organizer.

The students could do the activity on Learning Startegy Card 12, and/or think of a problem or issue about the environment or about anything else they are interested in and write a persuasive letter to an appropriate person or group asking for help/support. Remind them to anticipate readers' objections while they are planning/preparing the content of their letters. They could share their letters in small groups.

Language Workshop — Spelling

Blackline Master 25 • adding endings; y to i; im pattern

Explore and Discover

Use Blackline Master 25 and the **sort**, **share**, **discuss**, and **chart** procedure outlined on page 16 to work with the words.

In the discussion, first list the words with "y" as a short "i" and words with "im" as a syllable. Ask students to add other words with the same patterns. Then focus on root words, asking students to find words that have prefixes or suffixes. Talk about changes that were made when endings were added. Make word webs showing root words and derivatives.

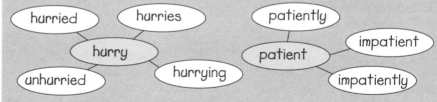

Follow this exploration with a **pretest**, **study and practise**, and a **post test** as outlined on page 16.

Study and Practise   Students could

• use Learning Strategy Card 3 to study words identified after the pretest.
• with a partner, make webs for words other than the ones done as a group. These webs can be put up on the bulletin board for other students to refer to.
• arrange their study cards under the following headings to create a matrix. They can copy the matrix onto paper and underline the spelling feature or pattern in each word. They could also add their own words to the list.

	"y" changed to "i"	silent "e"	"im"	"y" as a short "i"
2 syllables	hurried worried studied applied	announced	impact	crystal
3 syllables			impatient important	mystery
4 syllables			impossible	gymnasium

Oral Communication

Discuss an Issue

Recall with students how the meeting nearly got out of hand because the people were discussing something that they had strong feelings about. Ask the students to brainstorm some guidelines for a discussion about an issue so that this kind of thing wouldn't happen. Ask them to also think about what participants could do to convince others of their point of view. Record their ideas.

The discussion format outlined here is designed as a first step toward formal debating.

Have students brainstorm and list issues, as statements, that they feel strongly about and would like to discuss. The list might include topics such as:
- All restaurants should be non-smoking.
- No girls should play on a boys' hockey team.
- No one should be allowed to own a gun.
- There should be curfews for children under sixteen.

DISCUSSING AN ISSUE

- Everyone gets to talk without interruption.
- Everyone listens carefully to everyone else.
- No one is rude to others because of what they say.
- Speakers should plan what they will say.
- Speakers should give reasons for their opinions.
- No one 'wins' the discussion.

Organize the students into groups of four to six and invite them to choose an issue they wish to discuss from the list. Ask the students to decide independently whether they are for or against the issue and consider the points they would like to make to the group. Some students may wish to jot down their points before the discussion.

The students can number off in their groups, and, beginning with number one, proceed around the circle sharing how they feel about the issue and stating their key points in support of their opinion.

As a whole group, discuss the value of the discussion, talking about whether anyone changed or modified their ideas after listening to others.

 See **Assess Learning**, page 97.

LINK TO CURRICULUM

Language Arts

Plan a Meeting

Students could work in small groups to plan a classroom meeting about an issue pertaining to their classroom or school to see how the problem could be solved. Suggest that they plan the tasks that need to be done before, during, and after the meeting, and designate who is responsible for completing each task.

Each group could share its plans with the class to receive feedback about the steps and revise their plans accordingly.

Find and Read a Variety of Materials

Students could look through the school library, public library, and their homes to find books, magazines, or newspapers that have stories and articles on environmental issues in their community, province, and around the world.

Give students an opportunity to share their reading discoveries with the class, to talk about what they learned about different issues, and which materials they like best and why. This could be done for five to ten minutes a day.

Science

Research an Ecosystem

Pairs of students could identify and research a particular ecosystem. They could use library resources and computer resources such as CD-ROMs and the Internet. (See pages 5 and (ii) for more information.) Suggest that the focus of their research could be the links among the different organisms in the ecosystem.

They could document their findings in a fact sheet, or they could create a diorama of their ecosystem to present to the class.

The Arts

Design a Bulletin Board

Ask the students to discuss how information about the problems in our environment could be shared by creating a bulletin board display to provide a message for others. The display could show problems as well as examples of how problems are being addressed.

Suggest that they examine the bulletin boards around the school or recall ones that have impressed them, and, together with three or four classmates, plan their design. If possible, provide each group with a space to create a bulletin board display.

Assess Learning

Assessment

Oral Communication (see p. 97)

Following the discussion, ask students to do a **self-assessment** about their participation by answering the following questions on a piece of paper.

• Did you express your ideas clearly and without anger?
• Did you give reasons for your opinion?
• Were you respectful of classmates' points of view? How did you show this?
• Did you find that you learned more about the issue by hearing others' viewpoints? Give an example.
• What did you find most valuable about the group discussion?

Use this opportunity to conference individually with a few students to praise their involvement in the group discussion and coach those who might benefit from a review of the criteria for sharing points of view.

Worldly Wise

Through two reflective poems by Maxine Tynes, students are invited to think about the world's environment and other issues and how they can play a role in making the world a better place to live.

Anthology, pages 78-79

Key Learning Expectations

Students will
• begin to identify a writer's point of view **(Reading Focus, p. 99)**
• read a variety of fiction and non-fiction materials for different purposes **(Reading Mini Lesson, p. 100)**
• communicate ideas and information for a variety of purposes **(Writing Mini Lesson, p. 100)**
• create a variety of media works **(Visual Communication Mini Lesson, p. 101)**

LINK TO EXPERIENCE

Explore World Problems

Have the students brainstorm a list of world problems. As well as environmental concerns, encourage them to think of problems that include ways we treat and behave toward others.
Some of their ideas might include
• oil spillage in the oceans
• killing of animals to the point of extinction
• homeless people
• starving children in the world
• destruction of forested areas in the world

Have the students work in small groups to categorize the list of problems and give each category a title. Then ask them to number the categories in order of priority, with number one being the most important to the group. Have each group share the category they felt was priority one and give reasons for their choice.

Write About a World Problem

Students could write in their journals about a problem in the world that they are most concerned about. Encourage them to write about why this problem is important to them and what they think should or could be done to solve it. They could share their writing with a partner, if they wish.

READ AND RESPOND TO TEXT

Reading Focus

Using the **read and reflect** strategy, the students can read the poems independently or listen to the *COLLECTIONS 5* audio version to determine the message. Then, with a partner, they can discuss these questions:
• What is the author telling you in these poems?
• Do you think these messages relate to you? Why or why not?

As a group, have the students share their thoughts about the poet's messages and find phrases that reflect the message, such as save a lake, keep peas and carrots fresh, clean up the streets, and so on.

Invite the students to read the poems to themselves again to find the stanza that best reflects their personal feelings and thoughts. Ask volunteers to read these stanzas to the group and share why the stanza is important to them.

Reader Response

Students could
• hold a conversation about the poems with a partner or in a small group, using questions such as:
  – **What kind of person do you think the author of these poems is? Why?**
  – **Are you like her in any way? How?**
  – **What is your reaction to the messages of the poems?**
  – **Do you agree with what is said about the situation of the world? Why or why not?**
  – **If you were the author, what would you have added to the message in the poems?**
• find an article in the local newspaper that addresses one of the concerns talked about in the poems.
• choose a phrase or stanza from one of the poems and draw an accompanying illustration.
• write about a personal experience that is brought to mind by something in the poems.
  • talk with a family member(s) about things in the poems they do not understand.

Get Ready to Read

Ask students, if they could change one thing in the world for the better, what it would be and why. Then tell them that in this selection, they will read two poems about what needs to be done to make our world a good place to live.

 **R EVISIT THE TEXT**

Reading

Web the Main Idea in Poems

Ask students to suggest a word or phrase that captures the most important message shared in both of the poems.

> problems of the world

> wake up and beware

> the world needs your help

> environmental concerns

Have them choose the one they think is best and write it in the centre of the board or on an overhead transparency. Have students revisit the poem to find words or phrases that support the main idea to make a web.

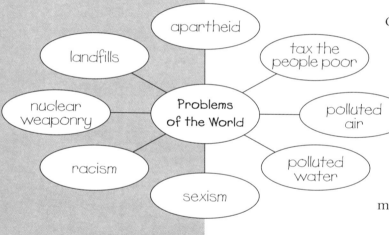

Conclude by helping students understand that one way that they have of interpreting a poem is to think about a word that describes the main idea, and then to look in the poem for words and phrases that connect to it.

Have students look for one or two other poems from their personal reading and create a web showing the main idea and supporting words and phrases.

Writing

Write a Slogan

Ask students to brainstorm interesting slogans that they are familiar with. Examples could include: "Just Do It" from Nike, "Be All That You Can Be" from the Army, "Hot Eats Cool Treats" from Dairy Queen, "We Want To Be Your Store" from Eatons, and "Always Be Prepared" from the Girl Guides.

Talk about what makes a slogan appealing. Help the students identify that a slogan is successful when it
• is short.
• grabs your attention through rhyme, alliteration, play on words, style of lettering, ….,.
• links the right words with the idea.
• persuades your thinking on an idea.

Display a number of headlines from newspapers about problems in the community and/or the world. Have students examine the headlines and choose one to write a slogan for that offers a cure for the problem. Show them an example to help them get started.

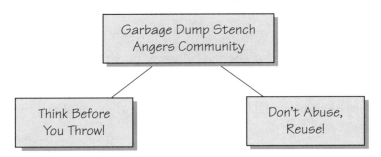

Garbage Dump Stench
Angers Community

Think Before
You Throw!

Don't Abuse,
Reuse!

Students could share their slogans with the group to get feedback on them, then write them on strips of paper, like bumper stickers, and display them in the classroom or school hallway.

Visual Communication

Choose Photos/Illustrations to Represent Messages

Have the students examine the illustration in the anthology, and with a partner, discuss how the picture captures the message of the poems, using questions such as the following:
• What do you think of when you look at the illustration?
• What in the illustration reminds you of the poems? Why?
• If you were the illustrator, what would you have pictured to represent the messages in the poems?

Ask partners to share their ideas with the class.

Invite students to revisit the poems and choose one of the lines/phrases that appeals to them such as: "Keep the Bay of Fundy Blue…" or "Recycling's cool, and a life-saver, too!" Have them look through magazines and newspapers to choose appropriate photographs or other artwork that illustrate their choices. The pictures could be cut out and pasted on sheets of paper, and students could write captions for them. Some students may choose to create their own illustrations.

The photographs and illustrations could be compiled and made into a Big Book and shared with other classes in the school. Also, the students may wish to take the book home to share with their families. This could be done on a rotational basis.

Remind students to get permission before cutting out any pictures.

Assessment   See **Assess Learning**, page 103.

LINK TO CURRICULUM

Language Arts

Collect Poems and Songs

Students could look for poems and songs about the environment. The material could be about their community, country, and the world. The poems and song lyrics could be copied and displayed for everyone to enjoy. Or recordings of the song could be put in the Listening Centre.

Social Studies

Identify and Locate World Problems

The students could make their own personal statements of how they will be a watcher of the world. Their statement should include what the problem is and what they are going to do to watch and help solve the problem. They could write their statements on file cards and pin them to the appropriate spots on an outline map of the world or Canada. Some locations and problems could concern:
– rain forests in South America
– racial tension in South Africa
– the homeless in Canadian and American cities
– fishing in the Maritimes

Students may wish to liaise with another school via Internet and exchange information about their particular concerns.

Find Out About Canada's Environment Policy

Have the students work in small groups to outline the steps they could follow to find out what Canada's policy is to preserve the environment. Have them brainstorm the approaches they might take in acquiring this information. They might suggest:
– doing research in the public library
– writing or faxing Environment Canada
– locating information via Internet
– telephoning environment activist groups

Once the information has been gathered, the students could outline the key points of the policy and display them.

 Some students may want to access software programs such as *Earth's Natural Resources* or encyclopedia CD-ROMS to find out about world problems. (See pages 5 and (ii) for more information.)

The Arts

Design a Poster

Invite students to work independently to design a poster entitled "Here's What You Can Do to Help!" The poster would depict an activity where children are helping in some way to make the world a better place to live.

Display the posters and ask each student to explain the main message of the poster. The posters could be displayed in a school hallway or the library.

Assess Learning

Visual Communication (see p. 101)

Use the viewing/representing activity as a sample of **peer assessment**. Pair the students, and as each partner examines the others' choice of photographs and illustrations, they can make a written comment on
– the information that each photograph/illustration
  gave to the viewer
– how well they think the photographs/illustrations
  matched the chosen problem

The comments should be dated, signed, and attached to the sheet of photographs/illustrations. These could be stored in the students' portfolios.

Anthology, page 80

Our Environment — *a commentary*

Pollution — *a poem*

Animals — *an opinion*

STUDENT WRITING

LINK TO THE THEME

After reading the selections, students could
• make categorized lists of words from the student writing that are connected to environmental concerns, choose a list, and write the words in a shape or line poem.

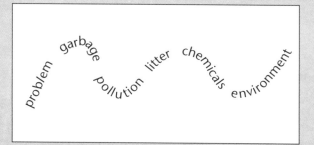

problem garbage pollution litter chemicals environment

• in small groups, talk about connections they see between the student writing pieces and any other selections in the anthology.

LINK TO THE WRITING PROCESS

Respond to a Challenge or Question

Have students skim the selections to note the concluding challenge or questions of each: "...we can make a difference!" "When is someone going to care?" "What would our world be like without animals?" Ask them to choose one of these areas of concern and write a paragraph expressing what they think they could do to help. The paragraphs could be shared and posted.

Language Workshop — Grammar

• use correctly the conventions of grammar (adjectives)

Blackline Master 21

Teach/Explore/Discover

To illustrate how precise vocabulary clarifies meaning and helps create accurate and/or vivid images, write the words "cars," "bottles," "tires," and "boxes" on the board. Invite students to brainstorm descriptive words (adjectives) that could describe these things (nouns). Talk about the images these adjectives bring to mind. Then ask them to find the adjectives that describe these words in the student writing and note how each adjective made them the image that the author wanted, not one of their own making. Elicit from the students that it is important to choose adjectives carefully so the readers see the images that they, as authors, want them to see.

Practise/Apply

Students could

• complete Blackline Master 21, *Descriptive Words.*

• choose a story or poem that has good descriptive words and read a particularly effective section to a partner.

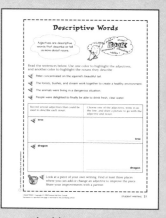

Blackline Master 21

LINK TO THE WRITER

After reading about Neel's method of preparation for writing, students can look through their writings to note when they have applied similar methods, and how their writing was affected. If they have had no such experience, they can choose a topic, then jot notes for the five Ws and the H, in preparation for writing a non-fiction piece.

Using the Genre Books and Novels

Learning Expectations

Students will

1. Read a variety of fiction and non-fiction materials for different purposes.

2. Explain their interpretation of a written work, supporting it with evidence from the work and from their own knowledge and experience.

3. Identify various forms of writing and describe their characteristics.

4. Select appropriate reading strategies.

Strategies for Book Connections and Study

Literature Response Journal

Students can write in their journals following the first reading or keep notes throughout the reading experience.

Suggest that they write
- impressions about the story or the characters.
- questions about parts they didn't understand.
- notes about things that surprised them.

Reading Workshop

Following the first reading, ask students who read the same book to form small workshop groups. They could begin by
- talking about their favorite parts of the book.
- posing questions about parts they didn't understand or that surprised them.

Guide each group to develop a collaborative plan for focusing their workshops over a few days.

Approaching the Books

- Arrange the students in four groups, with each group reading a different book.
- Students could preview the books to self-select the one that they would like to read or read the book that best fits their reading level (see pages 6–7).
- Following the book "study," the groups could exchange books and read the other books as part of personal reading if they wish.

PACING TIP

Use the books as a group book exploration and study during the last two weeks of the unit.

Our Reading Workshop Plan

Day 1 – Discuss characters
- Who are they?
- What are they like?
- Who do they remind us of?

Day 2 – Discuss plot
- What surprised us in the plot?
- Did the plot turn out the way we thought it would?
- How would we change the plot?

Day 3 – Share reactions
- We'll take turns sharing and discussing together our journal notes.

Day 4 – Read aloud our favorite parts

The Reader Response activities in each teaching plan provide other ideas for workshops.

The Hundred Penny Box

This touching book-length story by Sharon Bell Mathis tells of a young boy's love for his great-great aunt. Michael's hundred-year-old aunt has a box of pennies, one for each of her birthdays, and a favorite pastime for Michael is listening to his aunt tell the story behind each penny. This story relates most closely to the unit topic focus of person to person (see pages 6-7).

INTRODUCING THE BOOK
Recall a Personal Experience

Ask the students to recall when they spent an extended period of time with an older relative or friend. Have them discuss
- how they felt about having an older person around
- special or different things they had to do
- things that they found difficult
- what they liked about spending time with an older person

The students' ideas could be charted under these four headings: Feelings, Special Duties, Challenges, and Good Things. As they read the story, they can check the chart to see which of their ideas are similar to those in the story.

Recall "A Morning to Polish and Keep"

Review the selection "A Morning to Polish and Keep" (*Together Is Better*, p. 4) and talk about the souvenirs the children chose because they were special to them and would remind them of the fishing trip. Invite the students to think of an item they have saved because it reminds them of something that they don't want to forget. Ask them to draw the item and then list next to the picture words and phrases that tell about their item.

Have pairs of students share their picture and, using the words and phrases as a guide, tell why their saved item is important and what memories it evokes.

CONNECTING WITH THE BOOK
Explore Book Features

Prior to reading, ask the students to look at the book and note features such as the following:
- the cover and title page (publisher, author, and illustrator)
- the dedication page (the people the author wants to pay tribute to)
- the page featuring a quote

Using this information, invite students to predict what they think the book might be about.

Reading Focus

Using the **read and connect** strategy, pairs of students could read the story together, taking turns reading aloud, or some students may prefer to read the book independently.
(See Activity 1.)

> Activities on the next two pages serve as guides to focus students' reading and response. The pages can be duplicated and made into transparencies, response sheets, or activity cards.

A SUGGESTED APPROACH TO READING THE BOOKS

Provide time for at least two readings:

First Reading

The main goal of the first reading is to provide students with a satisfying reading experience along with a general understanding of the book.

Students who are at the **fluent stage** could read the entire text on their own, pausing to discuss portions of the text as they wish.

Students who would benefit from more **guidance** could use the strategy targeted for the selection.

Further Readings

As students engage in further readings, they will deepen and extend their understanding and appreciation through a more detailed exploration of the book.

Read *The Hundred Penny Box*

In this story, Michael has a special relationship with his Great-Great-Aunt Dew. Read the story with a partner or on your own. Then read and think about what you will write in each box below and write your responses.

Explain how Michael feels about his Aunt Dew. Find some words and phrases in the story to support your opinion. Why do you think he feels this way?

Explain your reactions to Michael's mom wanting to throw away Aunt Dew's penny box. Writing your reasons for the way you felt will help explain your answer.

Explain what you think Aunt Dew meant when she said, "Them's my years in that box. That's me in that box."

The Hundred Penny Box
☐ make judgements and draw conclusions about the content in written materials, using evidence from the materials

READER RESPONSE

 Design Illustrations

Imagine that the illustrators of this book have asked you to design two more illustrations for the book. Choose two parts of the story that really appeal to you and draw the illustrations to match the story. You could copy the style of the pictures in the book or you can draw them in any way that you want.

The Hundred Penny Box

 Discuss the Story

With three other classmates, find a quiet spot to discuss the story. Assign yourselves numbers from 1 to 4. The person with the number 1 begins the discussion, and the other group members add their comments in turn. You can use these questions to guide your discussion.

- Was there a time when you felt like Michael? What happened to make you feel that way?

- When you are upset or sad about something, do you react as Michael did in the story? Or do you deal with upsetting things in other ways?

- What did you learn from reading this story?

- If you were the author of this story, what would you change? Why?

The Hundred Penny Box

 Dramatize a Conversation

Aunt Dew and Michael had many interesting conversations throughout the story. With a partner, look through the book and choose your favorite conversation between the two. Role-play the conversation, adding any dialogue that you wish. When you are ready, show your dramatization to some classmates.

The Hundred Penny Box

 Create a Memory Box

What special memories do you have? What do you have or wish you had to remind you of those memories? Decorate a special box and put in objects or drawings of your "memory reminders." If you want to, share your box and its contents with a classmate, telling about each object and why it is special.

The Hundred Penny Box

 Tape and Write Stories

Is there someone in your family who tells stories that you love to hear? Tape-record one of the stories. Then listen to the tape and write down the story. Check the story for spelling and neatness. Draw some illustrations for the story and give it to the person who told you the story.

The Hundred Penny Box

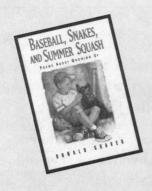

Baseball, Snakes, and Summer Squash

In this collection of free verse poems, Donald Graves provides a look at his experiences as a young boy at home and in school, most of them about his life after his family moved out to the country from their city apartment. These personal accounts relate most closely to the unit topic focus of special moments and memories (see pages 6-7).

INTRODUCING THE BOOK

Write About a Recent Experience

Invite students to think back over the past year or so and recall an experience that stands out in their minds. Suggest that they first jot down the important points of the experience, then write an anecdote telling about it. They can then read their anecdotes to a partner and talk about their experiences.

Recall "Moments and Memories"

Ask students to think back on or skim over "Moments and Memories" (*Together Is Better*, p. 12), to recall that each of the authors related an important experience he or she had with family or friends. Explain that in the book *Baseball, Snakes, and Summer Squash*, the author relates some of his childhood experiences in free verse poetry (poems without rhyme or rhythm patterns). As they read the poems, suggest that they think about the differences and similarities between describing personal experiences in prose and in poetry.

CONNECTING WITH THE BOOK

Explore Book Features

Prior to reading, ask the students to look at the book and note features such as the following:
- the cover and title page
- information about the author and the book
- copyright page with a sentence summary about the book and information about the drawings
- the table of contents, noting the large number of poems
- pencil drawings to illustrate some poems

Invite students to read the titles of the poems in the table of contents and talk about which of the experiences the author writes about might relate to themselves, and why.

Reading Focus

Students could use a **double look** strategy to first look over the poems and then choose some to read and share with others. **(See Activity 1.)**

Activities on the next two pages serve as guides to focus students' reading and response. The pages can be duplicated and made into transparencies, response sheets, or activity cards.

Read *Baseball, Snakes, and Summer Squash*

When he was in grade four, Donald Graves moved with his younger brother and his parents from their apartment in the city to a home in the country. In this collection of poems, he tells about experiences with his family and at school in grades four and five.

Read the first two poems to learn something about Donald's experiences in the apartment and about his move to a country home. Talk with a partner about what you think it would be like to live in each of these places.

Then look through the table of contents and pick out five poems you think look interesting. Read those poems to yourself and try to picture what Donald is telling you about.

You could work with a partner to do one or more of these activities.

> Choose a favorite poem to read aloud to each other.

> Talk about the poems you each read.
> — Did you read any of the same poems?
> — Were the poems about what you expected from reading the title?
> — What did you like or dislike about the poems?

> Check to see where the poems you both read come in the table of contents. Can you see a pattern to when the poems took place when you think about the different poems you and your partner read?

Now try this...

Go back to the table of contents and look at it carefully. You now have a little idea of Donald's experiences, his friends and family, their pet, and things at school. Choose five more poems to read and share with your partner. Or you may want to read the whole collection.

Baseball, Snakes, and Summer Squash

☐ decide on a specific purpose for reading, and select the material that they need from a variety of appropriate sources

READER RESPONSE

 ## Write and Illustrate a Memory Poem

Donald Graves's poems could be thought of as personal journal entries because they tell about things that have happened in his life. Think of an experience of your own that you were reminded of while reading one of the poems. Write a free verse poem that tells about your experience. Read it over carefully, to check for spelling and to see if you can add any descriptive words. Then copy your poem neatly onto a sheet of paper and illustrate it with pencil drawings like those of the illustrator for the poems in the book.

Baseball, Snakes, and Summer Squash

Put the Poems in Groups

As you read through the poems, you can see that Donald is telling about memories he has of experiences with his family, their pet dog, his friends, and things at school. Using these ideas and others as headings, make a web or chart listing the poems under headings that tell what the poems are about.

Baseball, Snakes, and Summer Squash

 ## Illustrate a Poem

Draw a cartoon strip or a single illustration to show what one of the poems is about. You can include thought and speech balloons in your picture, write a few sentences about what is happening, or perhaps give your picture a title.

Baseball, Snakes, and Summer Squash

 ## Dramatize One of the Poems

With one or two other students who have read this poetry book, choose one of the poems to act out. Decide upon the character parts and what simple props you might like to use to help create the scene or action. Practise your dramatization before performing it for other students in the class. You might like to read the poem aloud after you've acted it out.

Baseball, Snakes, and Summer Squash

 ## Evaluate Your Handwriting

Reread the poem "Handwriting" to get an idea about Donald's handwriting. Look at Learning Strategy Card 13 and think about your own handwriting.

Choose a piece of writing you have just recently completed. It might be your memory poem, a story or letter you have written, notes in social studies or science, or your spelling dictation list. Look at your handwriting and ask yourself:

- Are the letters formed correctly?
- Do the letters all slant in the same way?
- Is the height of the letters even?
- Is the space between words big enough to separate one word from the other?
- Are the words not too far apart?
- Is the paper free of smudges and scribbled out letters?

Look at these two samples of writing. Which one do you think is better? Why?

Our family's baseball game was hilarious.

Our family's baseball game was hilarious.

You and a partner can check Learning Strategy Card 13, look at each other's handwriting together, then talk about the good points and ways the writing can be improved.

Baseball, Snakes, and Summer Squash

A Bad Case of Robots

This is a humorous story about a trio who get involved with a sensational machine—a robot that seems to know everything until things start to go wrong. This novel by Kenneth Oppel relates most closely to the unit topic focus of person to person (see pages 6-7).

INTRODUCING THE BOOK

Write a Journal Entry

Have the students write in their journals about a time when they organized something, made something, or tried an experiment that didn't turn out the way they had planned. Encourage them to write about how they felt as well as what went wrong. They could share their writing with a partner and talk about what they learned from the experience.

Recall "The Last Dragon"

Ask the students to recall or skim the story "The Last Dragon" (*Together Is Better*, p. 62) and identify the approach Peter used in trying to solve his problem of restoring the dragon. Ask them to discuss with a partner why they feel he was so successful. Suggest that they think about this when reading *A Bad Case of Robots* to compare the two stories.

CONNECTING WITH THE BOOK

Explore Book Features

Prior to reading, ask students to look over the book and note features such as the following:
- the cover and the title page (author, illustrator, and publisher)
- the dedication and copyright page
- the division into chapters
- the back page with information about the story

Invite students to talk about their first thoughts or impressions about the book.

Reading Focus

Students could use a variation of the **narrated reading** strategy to predict possible story events and actions of the characters.
(See Activity 1.)

> Activities on the next two pages serve as guides to focus students' reading and response. The pages can be duplicated and made into transparencies, response sheets, or activity cards.

Read *A Bad Case of Robots*

This novel tells the story of how an unusual invention, a robot, causes trouble for three children.

Use the chart below to guide you as you read through the story. First read the chapter grouping, then stop and predict what you think will happen next and what the characters will do before you read the next chapter grouping. At the end of each grouping, talk about how close your predictions were and share your new predictions with a classmate.

READ	PREDICT
Chapters 1 and 2	
Chapters 3, 4, and 5	
Chapters 6 and 7	
Chapters 8 and 9	

A Bad Case of Robots □ make judgements and draw conclusions about the content in written materials, using evidence from the material

READER RESPONSE

 Discuss Ways to Solve Problems

Think of a time when you worked in a group to complete a task. Divide a sheet in two. On one side, list some of the problems you experienced in getting the work done. On the other side of the sheet, list what you did to try and solve the problems. Share your sheet with a partner and talk about what might have been the best ways or other ways to solve the problem.

Some Problems	What I Did

A Bad Case of Robots

 Web a Character's Characteristics

Choose your favorite character and, using a web, describe his or her personality from the information you read in the story. Your web could include headings such as Likes/Dislikes, Habits, Appearance, and Hobbies. Share your web with a classmate and be prepared to provide proof for your ideas.

A Bad Case of Robots

 Design a Toy Robot or Special Machine

Imagine that a famous toy company has invited you to draw a detailed design for a toy robot or special toy machine. Along with the design, the company would like you to explain what the toy is able to do and why it would be a great toy to buy. Draw the design and write a letter to the toy company, explaining what they want to know. You might like to work with a partner on this project.

A Bad Case of Robots

 Write a Readers' Theatre Script

With a partner, rewrite one of the chapters into a Readers' Theatre script. Remember to include a narrator and the characters from the chapter. (You can use Learning Strategy Card II as a reminder of Readers' Theatre.)

A Bad Case of Robots

 Read About Experiments

Visit your school or public library to search for books, CD-ROMs, magazines, and information on the Internet about interesting experiments. Share with a classmate the funniest, most unusual, most interesting, or most complicated experiment you read about.

A Bad Case of Robots

How Come the Best Clues Are Always in the Garbage?

When money donated to an environmental group is stolen from their home, eleven-year-old Stevie Diamond sets out to catch the thief. She has many exciting and humorous adventures as she follows up on clues. This mystery novel by Linda Bailey relates most closely to the unit topic focus of working for a cause (see pages 6-7).

INTRODUCING THE BOOK

Talk About Mystery Books and Movies

Have students read the title of the book and suggest what type of story they think it will be. Ask them to tell what they like or dislike about stories of this type and to list mystery/detective books they have read or movies or TV programs they have watched. Students may wish to bring in some favorite mystery/detective books from home or the library for classmates to read.

Recall "Last Chance for Cherry Tree Creek"

Talk with students about the theme of this selection (*Together Is Better*, p. 71), bringing out the concern about the environment as related to the discovery of dead frogs at Cherry Tree Creek. Ask students to keep this in mind while reading *How Come the Best Clues Are Always in the Garbage?* to see what similarities there are between the two stories.

CONNECTING WITH THE BOOK

Explore Book Features

Prior to reading, ask students to look over the novel and note features such as the following:
- the cover and title page
- the copyright page with the acknowledgment and the disclaimer about the characters
- the dedication
- the division into chapters that are numbered but not named
- the summary of the book and information about the author

Invite the students to read the book summary and talk about how they think the title of the book and the summary tie together. They might consider such things as why clues would be in the garbage and what kind of clues to this robbery would be there.

Reading Focus

Students could use a **read and paraphrase** strategy, stopping at the end of each chapter or group of chapters to reflect on the setting of the story, the story events, and the characters. **(See Activity 1.)**

> Activities on the next two pages serve as guides to focus students' reading and response. The pages can be duplicated and made into transparencies, response sheets, or activity cards.

Read *How Come the Best Clues Are Always in the Garbage?*

In *How Come the Best Clues Are Always in the Garbage?* Stevie Diamond has many exciting and humorous adventures when she sets out to catch the thief who stole the money donated to an environmental group, the Garbage Busters.

Read the first chapter aloud with other students who are reading this novel. In a chart, describe the setting and the important events. Write a title for the chapter that tells the main idea, but doesn't give everything away.

> **Chapter:** 1   Title: *Stolen Money*
>
> **Setting:** *in Stevie (Stephanie) and her mom's house*
>
> **Important Events:** *the Garbage Busters' money (not the coins though) has been stolen from Stevie's house while her mom was bike riding with Jonathon. Stevie thinks about things: the weird phone calls, the …*

Read the rest of the story and complete the chart for each chapter on your own or with a partner. You might want to read the book in these sections:

Chapters 2 and 3	Chapters 9, 10, 11, and 12
Chapters 4, 5, and 6	Chapters 13, 14, and 15
Chapters 7 and 8	Chapters 16 and 17

How Come the Best Clues Are Always in the Garbage?   ☐ read a variety of fiction and non-fiction for different purposes

READER RESPONSE

 Describe Feelings

As you read the story, you likely experienced a variety of feelings. You might have been excited, scared, worried, relieved, confused, or disgusted. Fold a piece of paper into four parts. At the top of each part, write a heading describing one of the feelings you had. Then in each box, write about and/or draw a picture showing a part of the story that made you feel that way.

Example:

Scared	Confused
I was scared when Jessie and Stevie were in the back of Arnie's van and speeding along to who knows where. I didn't know what would happen to them when they were discovered.	

How Come the Best Clues Are Always in the Garbage?

3 Make a Poster

Make a poster that could have been put up around the housing co-op where Stevie and her mom live. The poster could be one that tells people about the robbery and asks for assistance in finding the thief, or it could be one the Garbage Busters would use to inform people of their concern about the packaging the Red Barn uses and the litter around the restaurant. (You can use Learning Strategy Card 10 when you're planning your poster.)

How Come the Best Clues Are Always in the Garbage?

4 Read a Chapter as Readers' Theatre

With others who have read this novel, decide upon a chapter that you would like to do as a Readers' Theatre. Practise your reading before presenting it to your class. (You can use Learning Strategy Card 11 as a reminder of how to prepare for and perform Readers' Theatre.)

How Come the Best Clues Are Always in the Garbage?

5 Write a Newspaper Article

One Vancouver newspaper said Stevie was "Vancouver's answer to Nancy Drew," and another one called her a "girl wonder." Write an article that might have appeared in one of these newspapers describing how Stevie solved the robbery . Be sure to include in your article:

- a title or heading; perhaps using one of the phrases from the book
- a good opening to catch the readers' attention
- the most important things that led to Stevie's uncovering of the thief's identity
- something to keep the readers' attention; perhaps humorous or exciting parts of her adventure
- a conclusion that brings things to a close

You may want to include a drawing to illustrate something in your article.

Read your article to another student who has also read the story to see if you reported the story correctly.

How Come the Best Clues Are Always in the Garbage?

6 Play a Character Guessing Game

Make a group with students who have read the novel. To prepare for the game, each player lists the names of the characters, along with jot notes about their appearance, things they did, and things they said. These notes will help make questions about the characters.

Each player then writes at least five questions that can be answered by giving a character's name. Write the questions on the front of individual game cards, and the answer on the back. To play the game, players take turns drawing question cards and scoring a point when they give the correct answer.

How Come the Best Clues Are Always in the Garbage?

Concluding Connections and Study for the Genre Books and Novels

1. Share Small Group Learnings

Provide time for each book connections and study group to
- share their book, through a book talk or dramatization.
- lead a discussion on the ideas and topics in the book.
- tell how their book connects to the *Together Is Better* anthology selections and to the ideas encountered in the unit.
- do an oral reading of a section of the book.
- share some of their Reader Response activities.

2. Hold a Whole Class Conversation

Help students synthesize and summarize the understandings they have about their books by choosing questions similar to the following ones. Encourage responses to each question from all members of all of the book connections and study groups.

Questions for discussion

- Do you like the title the author chose for the book? Why? Why not? What title would you have chosen?
- Does the book remind you of other novels or stories? How are they the same? different?
- What do you think the author is trying to tell you by writing the book? Why do you think so?
- If you could change any part of the book, what would it be? Why? What would you change it to?
- What do you think happened after the book ended?

You might choose one question a day for a period of five days to either begin or end the class. Post the question a day ahead of time so that students can prepare their ideas and draw upon specific references in their respective books.

3. Make a Personal Response

Provide writing prompts such as the following for the students. They could
- write a book review of one of the books and send it to a local bookstore or library for inclusion in a newsletter, brochure, or display.
- write a letter to one of the main characters describing their personal feelings about the book and what they learned from it.
- write a conversation between two characters from a book. The conversation could be about how the characters liked being part of the book or what they have to say about other characters in the book. The conversations could be funny, serious, or share important information.
- make an entry in their literature response journals or notebooks describing their personal feelings about one of the novels or genre books that they have read.

The students' writing could be assessed and placed in their portfolios as one record of their understanding of the book.

Assess the Unit

Throughout the unit, there are many opportunities for ongoing assessment and celebration of what students have learned and accomplished in guided mini lessons and in individual or small group activities.

Ongoing Observations

Consolidate ongoing observations that you have noted for each student using the "Ongoing Assessment" boxes, your observation of literature discussions, group discussions, …,.

Unit Assessment Checklist

Use the *Assess Working Style and Attitudes Assessment Master* (*Assessment Handbook*) to help you assess performance on attitudes. Use Appendix 1 (pp. 150-151) in this book to help you assess and record student performance.

Gather and Record Assessment Information and Data

1. Reading

Use the **Together Is Better** *Reading Passages Assessment Masters* (*Assessment Handbook*). Students can read and respond to either or both of the passages. The Handbook describes how to choose the passages, how to conduct the activity, and criteria for scoring.

2. Writing

Students could submit one piece of writing of their choice for assessment.

Procedures and criteria for assessing the writing can be found in the *Assessment Handbook*.

3. Sample of Students' Learning for Portfolios

Review and assess learning records such as the following:
- logs of books students have read (*Reading Log Assessment Master, Assessment Handbook*)
- spelling and vocabulary pretests and post tests
- writing portfolios, including pieces of writing started or completed
- displays, models, scientific diagrams, and artwork
- research reports ▶

ASSESSMENT SUGGESTIONS

The *COLLECTIONS 5 Assessment Handbook* contains many suggestions and reproducible forms to assist with assessment and evaluation.

- webs, charts, notes crafted by students
- tapes of oral reading, oral presentations, or reports
- assignments of work or worksheets demonstrating performance on specific literacy tasks (such as those identified in "Assess Learning" activities noted throughout the unit)

Choose samples that will remain in the assessment portfolio as a record of student performance on the unit. The *Portfolio Checklist Assessment Master* in the *Assessment Handbook* may help you synthesize your assessment of students' work samples.

4. Self-Assessment

Students could
- *write in their learning logs* what they learned about family relationships and working and playing with others.
- *write a self-assessment report or "can do" list* to describe what they have learned. They might benefit from using the *Thinking Back on the Unit Assessment Master* (*Assessment Handbook*) containing prompts or lead-in phrases to help them focus on aspects of their learning.

They can use what they have prepared to help them plan what skills they need to work on in the next unit.

5. Teacher-Student Conferences

Throughout the unit, take opportunities to talk with individual students to see how they are progressing in personal reading and writing. Use or adapt
- *Questions to Guide a Personal Reading Conference Assessment Master* (*Assessment Handbook*) to help you conduct a **reading conference.**
- *Questions to Guide a Personal Writing Conference Assessment Master* (*Assessment Handbook*) to help you conduct a **writing conference.**

AT THE END OF AN ACTIVITY OR UNIT

My Self-Assessment Report

It was easy to read <u>Baseball, Snakes, and Summer Squash</u>. The poems are short and interesting. It seemed like I knew Donald Graves. We could have been friends. I like baseball and fishing and snakes and riding my bike, too. I'm not crazy about squash. The way he described some things made me feel like I was right there and they were just like what happens to me.

The story "Don't Just Sit There, Get a Hobby" made me feel kind of the same way. I felt like the kid Ken could have been me. It was funny when the jars got mixed up. I wouldn't mind catching snakes. But I wouldn't want to give them to the university people because I don't know what they'd do with them.

I really liked learning about the kids who play basketball in their wheelchairs. They must work very hard to get so good. Basketball is hard enough on your feet! I am going to write to the Alberta Northern Lights and maybe get to meet some of the players by writing letters or e-mailing to them. I'd like to find out what other kinds of sports are played by people with disabilities because my little brother has some problems.

One of my favorite activities was checking our school and neighborhood for wheelchair accessibility. I borrowed a wheelchair and tried to go where I usually go. I didn't get far! I think more people have to be aware of what people in wheelchairs have to put up with, and learn how to help them. I made a chart of where I couldn't go in our school with a wheelchair. I am going to write a letter to our principal about it.

I had trouble writing a diamante poem. They look like they'd be easy to write, until you sit down to do it! I like them though, so I'll keep trying.

Blackline Masters

Spelling Words Masters

Together Is Better

Home Connections Newsletter

About the Unit

Our new unit in language arts is *Together Is Better.* For the next month or so, we'll be talking, reading, and writing about special memories and activities with family, caregivers, and friends. As we work together, the students will have many opportunities to reflect on relationships built with friends and family through shared experiences of fun, support, and team work.

You can help make these connections at home. Together, look through this newsletter and choose books to share and activities and homework projects to do.

Learning Goals

In this unit, your child will

- listen to, read, and talk about selections related to times together with family and friends.
- extend his/her use of questioning in gaining information.
- learn about the development of character in stories.
- write letters, narratives, and poems.
- learn to spell words from personal and class lists.

BOOK BAG

These stories are about families and friends doing things together. Look for one or more of these books at your local library for your child to read or to share together.

- *The Auction* by Jan Andrews. A young boy and his grandfather share memories and stories as they spend a last day and night on the grandfather's farm before everything is auctioned off.

- *The Moccasin Goalie* by William Roy Brownridge. Four best friends on the prairies live to play hockey. They maintain their friendships and mutual respect through disappointments and triumphs related to hockey.

- *City Green* by Dyanne DiSalva Ryan. In this picture book, a young girl spearheads a community garden project, and finds that neighborhood relationships flourish along with the garden.

- *The Macmillan Book of Baseball Stories* by Terry Egan, Stan Friedmann, and Mike Levine. This collection of true short stories and photographs gives glimpses into lives of big league players and memorable events in the history of pro-ball.

- *Who Took Henry and Mr. Z?* by Dave Glaze. In this novel, two young sleuths try to solve the disappearance of the grade five class's two lovable guinea pigs.

A Family Fun Night

Set aside an evening for the family and/or caregivers to get together for an evening of recollections. People can present their special memory by themselves or with others. They may choose to sing a song that reminds them of some special family occasion, put on a skit, show a series of slides or a video, draw pictures, or set up a display of photos or souvenirs.

Your child has been reading stories and poems about family and friends, and how their relationships develop as they do things together. Talk with your child about one of the selections that reminded him/her of something your family has done together.

Homemade Fun

Play a Family Trivia Game

Members of the family can make cards on which they ask a trivia question about your family—a holiday you've been on, some special celebration, an interesting fact about someone, …. Players divide up into teams, take turns pulling a question card, and receive points for correct answers.

Make a friendship bracelet

In one of the selections we read, club members make friendship bracelets. You might want to try this at home. Someone in your family may know how to make these, or you and your child can follow instructions in a craft book such as Friendship Bracelets by Camilla Gryski.

Talk Together

Find opportunities, like mealtime or when you're driving in the car, to talk about questions such as the following, that are related to our *Together Is Better* unit.

- Do you have something a relative has given you that you really treasure? What is it and what special meaning does it have?

- What is an important tradition in your family? How did it get started and why do you think it has been carried on?

- Have you and your friends ever organized a club? What kind of things did you do together and what do you think was special about your club?

- What do you think builds team spirit? Tell about a team you've been on and what things helped to build a spirit that drew the members together.

- Have you and your friends or family ever taken on a project with a cause? Tell what it was and why it was important to you and to others.

Homework Projects

Week 1 — Tell About a Favorite Time of Year

Talk with a member of your family or a friend and recall things you do together at different seasons of the year. Together, decide what is your favorite time and consider reasons why. Write your thoughts in a few paragraphs and perhaps add an illustration.

Week 2 — Make a "Special Times" Mobile

List about five special memories you have of times with your family or friends. Cut out cardboard shapes on which to draw or write about each of these memories. Hang these on different lengths of string from a decorated coat hanger.

Week 3 — Present an Athlete or Team

Choose a sports team or an individual athlete to research. Find out background information, statistics, interesting details,…, and put it all together in a display or presentation to share with your classmates.

Week 4 — Work on a Project

Carry out a project with family members or friends. It can be one to help others or working for a cause. At some point, stop and think about why this project is important and how it is making a difference. Tape-record or write down the thoughts of those involved in the project, and perhaps the people you are helping or influencing.

Action Verbs

Replace the underlined verbs in these sentences with stronger verbs that convey a clear image for the reader.

1. John <u>said,</u> "Help me, I'm scared."

_____

_____

2. Sally <u>cried</u> when the nurse gave her the needle.

_____

_____

3. With the wind <u>blowing</u> and the rain <u>falling</u>, the family <u>went</u> for shelter to escape the violent storm.

_____

_____

Write three sentences of your own in which strong and precise verbs are used.

4. _____

_____

5. _____

_____

6. _____

_____

7. Now examine a piece of your writing and replace weak verbs with strong verbs. Share your edited changes with a partner.

Writing Dialogue

Add the correct punctuation and capital letters to these sentences.

Speaker tags are verbs that describe how dialogue is spoken

1   I'm sorry said James that I didn't get a chance to say hello to her

2   Hey Ali do you want to play soccer asked Sarah we can go to the park

3   I hollered Mom I'm home as I opened the door

4   Don't give away the surprise Cheryl whispered

5   Jessie shouted wait for me but everyone had left

Write three pieces of dialogue that have the speaker tags in different places.

6   _____

      _____

7   _____

      _____

8   _____

      _____

 9   Choose a story you have written that uses dialogue. Rewrite the dialogue using more descriptive speaker tags and changing the placement of them. Share your revised writing with a classmate.

Adding Information

Put parentheses around aside comments that add extra information.

> An aside comment gives additional information and sometimes adds humor. It can be written in parentheses ( ) following the part it tells more about.

1. My aunt went around ringing a little bell an annoying sound that drove us all crazy.

2. We settled down and tried to go to sleep in our tent our uncle's snoring made our attempt rather unsuccessful.

3. That bear the one that ate tomorrow's breakfast and lunch was a big black bear.

4. Our camping trip the one I'll never forget was soon over.

In your notebook, add asides in parentheses to the following sentences. You can write your additional information as part of the sentence that is already there, or you can add another complete sentence.

5. My cousin cooked sausages over the campfire.

6. The canoe tipped and we all ended up in the water.

7. My brother let out a screech when he saw the spider.

8. She'd been waiting a long time for supper.

9. Look at a story or paragraph you have written. See if you can find places where you could add aside comments to add information or humor. Read the original and the revision to a partner. Talk about whether the changes have made your writing more interesting.

Read and Reflect

Use this grid to guide you as you read the story. At each stopping point, talk about the questions with your partner or group.

Read	Discuss
Read pages 30 to 33 to find out what the problem is.	• How did Joelle and Eli react to the move to the shelter? How did their mother react? • How are their reactions different? similar?
Read from page 34 to the middle of page 35 to find out how things went in the next while.	• Tell what happened at the bus stop with Joelle and Violet. • What difference do you think this will make for the two girls and how they adjust to living in the shelter?
Read the rest of page 35, then to the bottom of page 36 to find out what is meant by "one thing led to another."	• Tell about two things that happened at the shelter that seemed to give Joelle a rather nice feeling. • Why did Joelle let Mrs. Hoffner think she still lived in her old building?
Read to the end of the story to find out something surprising that happens.	• Joelle was scared about coming home late, and the people waiting for her at home were scared. What was different about their feelings? • What did Claudia think when she saw all the shelter people in the front row seats? How was that different from what Joelle thought?

The story ends with Joelle being thankful that she could call the people from the shelter "my folks," and was proud to have them there to watch her in the play. What do you think made her change her mind about the shelter folks?

Make a Pop-up Card (A)

What You Need
- a piece of paper, 21.5 cm x 28 cm.
- a pencil   • a ruler
- scissors   • glue

What You Do

1 Fold the paper in half and then in quarters. Open the paper so it is only folded in half.

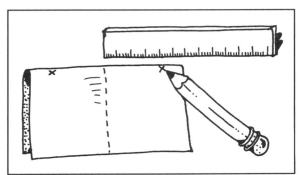

2 With the folded edge at the top, measure 8 cm from each side of the centre fold. Mark these points with an x.

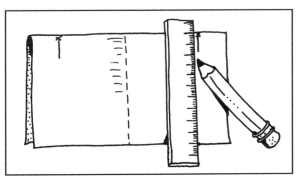

3 From each x, draw a vertical line 1.6 cm down.

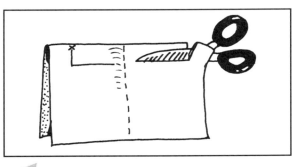

4 At the bottom of each line, draw a 6 cm horizontal line toward the centre fold. Cut along these lines.

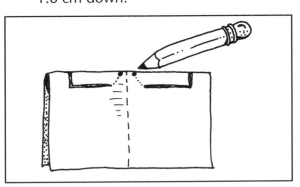

5 Measure 0.5 cm on either side of the centre fold and mark these points with a dot. Draw a dotted line from each dot to the end of each cut line.

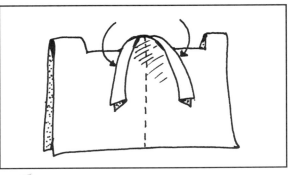

6 Fold the cut strips toward the centre, along the dotted lines. Press the folds firmly. Fold the cut strips back again.

Make a Pop-up Card (B)

What You Do (continued)

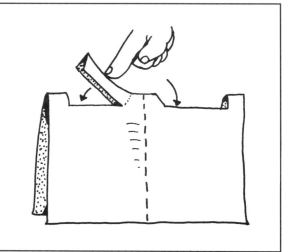

7. Stand your paper up like a tent. Push the strips through to the opposite side of the paper. Open the paper and press the folds of the strips in the opposite direction to the original folds. Close the paper and the strips should fold flat inside.

8. Apply glue around the edges of the back of your card and glue it to another piece of paper of the same size. Make sure you do not apply glue near the arms.

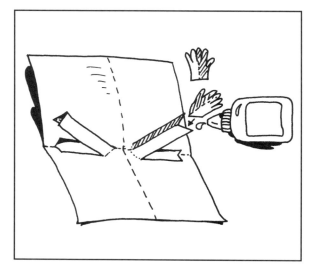

9. When you open your card, two arms will pop out. Cut out two hands, each about 3 cm long. Glue them to the arms and fold them along the same lines as the arm.

10. Draw and color a body, head, and legs to go with the arms. Write a personal message inside the card. Decorate the front of the card if you like.

Listening Behaviors/Skills

Student _____ Date _____

Listening Behaviors/Skills	1st	2nd	Comments/Improvements
The Listener: • looks at the speaker	☐	☐	
• stays still, doesn't fiddle or squirm	☐	☐	
• shows signs of interest: nods, smiles,…	☐	☐	
• doesn't interrupt	☐	☐	
• asks appropriate questions after the speaker finishes	☐	☐	
• makes appropriate comments after the speaker finishes	☐	☐	
• makes comments/questions that show that he/she remembered what was said	☐	☐	
• makes comments/questions that are related to what the speaker said	☐	☐	

A Note to Parents

MAY 12

DEAR PARENTS,

THIS IS JUST A LITTLE NOTE TO MAKE SURE YOU KNOW EVERYTHING ABOUT THE LITTLE KIDS' BASEBALL TEAM.

AS YOU PROBABLY KNOW WE ARE HOLDING PRACTISES IN THE FIELD BEHIND THE MAIL BOXES EVERY MONDAY AND FRIDAY 4:00 – 5:00. WE'D APPRECIATE IT IF YOU COULD GET YOUR CHILD(REN) TO AS MANY PRACTICES AS POSSIBLE. YOU WILL BE NOTIFIED IF A PRACTICE IS CANCELLED. WE MIGHT HAVE SOME GAMES AGAINST OTHER TEAMS BUT WE ARE NOT SURE YET. HOWEVER EVEN IF WE DON'T WE HOPE THAT THIS IS A GREAT LEARNING EXPERIENCE FOR YOUR CHILD(REN). WE WILL TRY TO MAKE IT AS SAFE AND FUN AS POSSIBLE FOR YOUR CHILD(REN).

WE WILL BE GETTING LITTLE UNIFORMS AND SOME EQUIPMENT, BUT TO GET THIS WE NEED TWO DOLLARS AND A PLAIN WHITE SHIRT PER CHILD. WE HOPE THIS IS NOT TOO MUCH AND WE WILL MAKE SURE THE MONEY GOES TO GOOD USE. PLEASE SEND THE MONEY TO THE NEXT PRACTICE ALONG WITH THIS FORM. IF YOU HAVE ANY FURTHER QUESTIONS PLEASE FEEL FREE TO PHONE ONE OF US WHOSE NUMBER IS ON THE CARD THAT IS ATTACHED. THANK YOU!

YOURS TRULY,

ANGELA DEAN

MATTHEW GINGRAS

STEPHANIE MEDFORD

CORRINE GINGRAS

BOBBY NICHOLS

- -

CHILD'S NAME _____

CHILD'S ALLERGIES _____

ANY CONCERNS OF PARENT _____

_____

PARENT'S SIGNATURE _____

All-In-One Thank You Letter

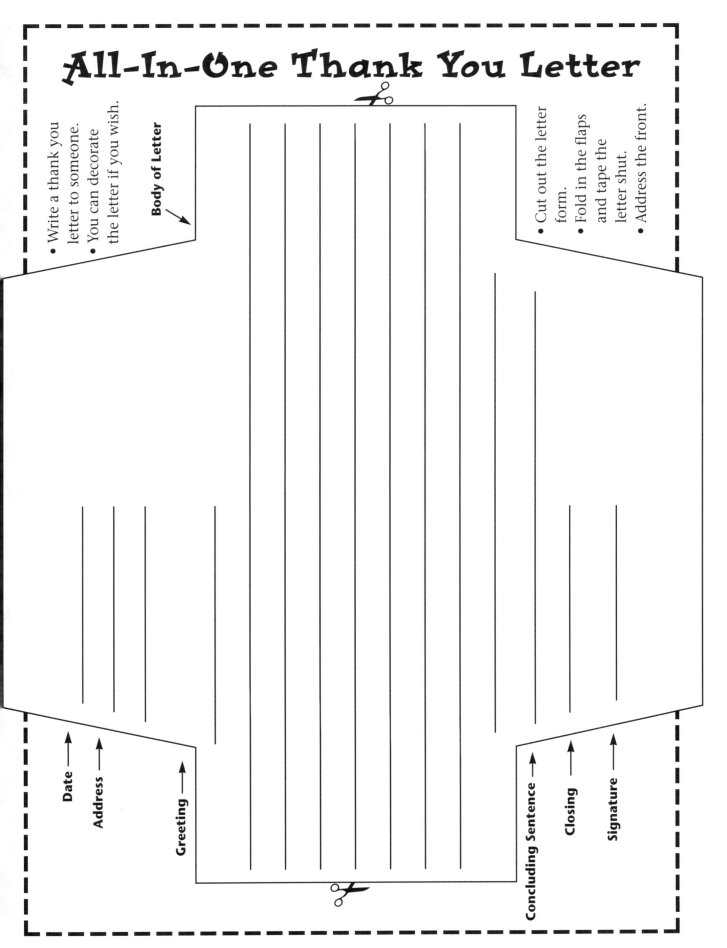

- Write a thank you letter to someone.
- You can decorate the letter if you wish.

Body of Letter

- Cut out the letter form.
- Fold in the flaps and tape the letter shut.
- Address the front.

Date

Address

Greeting

Concluding Sentence

Closing

Signature

Words in Capitals

The Sneeze

I winked and I blinked
And my nose got itchy
And my eyes all watered
And my mouth went twitchy
I went AHHHH
I went AHHHH
I went AHHHH **CHOOOOOO**
And I blew
And I sneezed
Then I coughed
And I wheezed
And my brother said, "Oh,
brother!"
And my mother said,
"GAZOONTIGHT!"
My father said, "Bless you!"
And I said, Ah… ah… ah…
AHHHHHHHHH **CHOOOOOOO**!

Sheree Fitch

ANXIOUS

Anxious
of course I'm anxious
afraid
of course I'm afraid
I don't know what about
I don't know what of
but I'm afraid
and I feel it's right to be.

Miriam Waddington

Read the poem "The Sneeze."

1. With a partner, talk about how the capitalized words added to the poem. Why do you think the author wrote some of the words in bold or darker letters?

2. Take turns reading the poem to each other. Use your voice to make the words in capital and bold letters sound dramatic.

Now read the poem "Anxious."

3. On your own, choose words that you would write in capitals if you were the author. Compare the words you chose with what your partner decided upon, and talk about your choices.

4. Take turns reading the poem aloud, with each of you using your voice to emphasize the words you selected.

Look through stories and poems you have written to see if there are any words you could write in capitals to emphasize something important.

Hot Wheels and Hoops

Young student triumphs as wheelchair basketball player

Just down the street and around the corner, an eight-year-old basketball player shoots hoops from his wheelchair.

Wainwright's Alexander Curtis debuted on the High School court along with other Mini Lights on Saturday, May 7. His parents, Frank and Sharon, and younger brother Andrew, were there to cheer him on.

Played soccer on crutches

Frank Curtis explained his son's affliction as spina bifida, at birth, restricting Alexander's mobility, and resulting in several operations already in his young life. "He always liked sports. He played soccer when he was 5, on crutches. When the soccer season was over, he asked, *What next, baseball?* Frank couldn't see himself running the bases for Alexander's every hit, so he looked for an alternative.

At the time, the family lived in Sherwood Park, and attended an exhibition game of "Northern Lights" wheelchair basketball. Alexander was enthused, but still too young to join the team. Mini Lights members are between the ages of 6 and 13 years. So Alexander waited it out, and joined the next season.

Regular Saturday practices

Shortly afterwards, Frank was transferred to Wainwright. Since that time, it's been a weekly outing to take Alexander to Sherwood Park for practices each Saturday from September to May.

At first, the novice player felt his efforts in his hands and arms, but practice strengthened his muscles. He learned his chair skills rapidly, practised his tosses into a garbage can at first, then a lowered hoop. Being the smallest on the team, it's a workout to play the regulation size court, but the 2-year veteran appears to thrive on the challenge.

"...a lot of fun..."

Alexander described Saturday's activity: "We played half of the team against half of the team. We had colored uniforms." He said he never got a basket, but it was a lot of fun anyways. (After the game he even took a baby for a spin in his wheelchair!)

Alexander doesn't feel terribly restricted by having to use a wheelchair. He hasn't quite mastered "wheelies" as yet, but he's sure trying.

"I'm No Hero"

Canadian completes global trek by wheelchair

In the summer of 1973, in British Columbia, Rick Hansen and a friend were riding in the back of a pickup truck. On a stretch of rough washboard road, the driver lost control and the truck flipped over. Both boys were thrown free. His friend escaped uninjured, but Rick landed on a metal toolbox and broke his back. In a few seconds, a healthy, athletic, confident kid of fifteen became a paraplegic—permanently paralyzed from the waist down.

Only seven months after the accident, Rick left the rehabilitation centre and drove himself home in a car equipped with hand controls. Rick tackled one challenge after another, achieving success at several levels. He went back to high school to get his diploma. Then he attended the University of British Columbia and graduated with a B.A. degree in physical education—the first disabled person ever to do so.

Training and Winning

At school and after graduation he participated in wheelchair sports. He played wheelchair basketball with a Vancouver team. He trained for racing events and became a world-class wheelchair marathon champion.

But Rick Hansen's real dream was to complete an around-the-world wheelchair tour to raise money for spinal-injury research and to focus world attention on the problems of disabled people.

Wheeling Around the World

On March 21, 1985, Rick Hansen set off on his journey around the world—a distance of 40 073 km—from Vancouver.

He faced unimaginable hardships: injuries, strong headwinds, rain, cold, going up and down mountains, sickness, thieves, mechanical problems. He kept going—through the United States, through countries in Europe, the Middle East, on to Australia and New Zealand.

On April 12, 1986, he sat atop the Great Wall of China. Then he started toward home—through Shanghai, South Korea, Japan, up the east coast of the United States, and finally into Canada, in Newfoundland.

Hometown Rally

The journey across Canada took nine months, because of the many stops and personal appearances, interviews, and banquets. In Williams Lake, B.C., where he grew up, the whole town showed up at a rally in his honor. "I'm just trying to do all I can," he told the crowd. "I'm no hero."

After more than two years, over 40 000 km, and 34 countries, Rick Hansen arrived back in Vancouver. He had reached both his goals: he had raised $20 million for spinal research and had increased public awareness of the problems and the potential of disabled people everywhere. Best of all, he personally inspired many disabled people with his courage and perseverance.